Advance Praise for *On the Shoulders of Atlas*

"I highly recommend *On the Shoulders of Atlas* for families planning the sale of their family business. For me it was déjà vu, as I worked with many of the same professionals and had the same concerns as Victor and Anne during the process. The book is enjoyable to read, and readers will find it easy to relate to the Banks family."
— *Ron Besse*
President & CEO, Gage Learning Corporation Ltd.

"*On the Shoulders of Atlas* clearly illustrates the advantages of pulling together the right team of professionals to secure the dreams of present and future generations. A must-read for anyone with a family business in transition."
— *Tracey Brophy*
Former President and CEO, Shred-it International Inc.

"This thought-provoking book brings back memories of selling a majority of my own business five years ago. A team approach for advisors is absolutely critical for a successful divestiture."
— *Marc Campbell*
Former CEO, Plastic Moulders Limited

"Running or being part of a family business is not always easy—or intuitive. We need to use modern advice and tools to promote succession of the business and the family. There are many times when the leader of a family business should ask for outside professional assistance. I have used many of the professionals who are part of this book and would recommend them wholeheartedly to any member of any family business."
— *Dan Greenberg*
  President, Ferguslea Properties Limited

"*On the Shoulders of Atlas* is almost like having a personal GPS device that leads you to your desired life destination."
— *Mark Leon*
  President, Lewmanic Investments Inc.

"I like business reports that fit on one page, but each page of this book made me want to read the next. *On the Shoulders of Atlas* shows how important it is for business families to get advice from professional advisors. I have recommended this book to every member of my family."
— *Jack May*
  Co-Founder, Maple Lodge Farms

"Transitioning a family-owned business can pose daunting challenges. *On the Shoulders of Atlas* lays out obtainable goals to a secure succession plan using an open and methodical approach while also engaging the very real and emotional concerns of the family. A must-read for any family in a family business."
— *Kim Mihalcheon*
  Executive Director, Steel-Craft Door Products Ltd.

"*On the Shoulders of Atlas* is an invaluable resource for anyone who wants to sell shares in a private company. I was fortunate to have several of the authors advising me when I sold my shares in Bulk Barn Foods. They held my hand every step of the way, ensuring the process was both easy and painless."
— *Maureen Ofield*
  Former owner, Bulk Barn Foods Ltd.

"Our parents founded our company in 1946 and my brother and I have been responsible for it for the past 50 years. Like Victor in *On the Shoulders of Atlas*, we considered a sale to a private equity fund but decided against it. I enjoyed reading the story of how one family dealt with all the decisions surrounding the sale of a family business. This book is a great guide to the many issues involved and to the available resources in addressing family business succession."
— *Tom Pick*
Chairman, Pickseed Companies Group

"*On the Shoulders of Atlas* explains key succession challenges very well. Anyone who has faced these challenges knows that a process like the one the authors describe is essential for avoiding the catastrophic losses caused by lack of planning."
— *Ken Reucassel*
Third-generation owner and President, The International Group, Inc.

"For over 150 years as a family business we have learned many of the valuable lessons contained in this informative book, sometimes the hard way. I recommend *On the Shoulders of Atlas* to anyone looking for insight as they face the many challenges that can present themselves when family businesses are in transition."
— *Hartley Richardson*
President and CEO, Richardson Financial Group

"With dead-on observations and vital advice, *On the Shoulders of Atlas* is the key to a successful transition to the next generation. Any entrepreneur considering retirement should take its lessons to heart. Having gone through the process myself, I can attest to the wisdom of the authors' work."
— *Joseph L. Rotman*
Chair, Roy-L Capital Corporation

"Management issues . . . tax issues . . . family issues. You might not have a clue how to solve all these issues, but the authors of *On the*

Shoulders of Atlas do. This book reflects an unmatched depth of knowledge and experience."
— *Herb Singer*
Founder and President, Discount Car and Truck Rentals

"Over the past 35 years, I've heard thousands of great stories about financial advisors providing extraordinary service to their clients. They all have several common features: the clients were almost always entrepreneurs, usually dealing with the complex issues of their multi-generational business families; the financial advisors invariably worked successfully as a team with the clients' other advisors; and the solutions created by these advisory teams always brought great, lasting value to dozens of individuals involved with the clients. The authors here do a great job of showing how their specialized knowledge and skills contribute to the overall team-work needed to transform the financial, succession, and legacy issues that business families cannot deal with on their own."
— *Dan Sullivan*
Founder, The Strategic Coach Inc.

"I wish there had been a book like this when I was going through the sale of our business!"
— *Ron Waters*
Former Vice Chairman, CHUM Limited

"A timely, thought-provoking story that captures all of the elements to be considered for the successful transition of a family business from generation to generation."
— *Thomas W. Bosley*
President and CEO, Bosley Real Estate Ltd.

"A must-read book for family businesses, families in transition, accountants, money managers, and other professionals working in the field of wealth management. It will also serve as an excellent case study for students in business and law, particularly students

in wealth management programs. The take-away from this book is that various options are available to families in transition, and that professional support is out there to help them choose the ones best suited to their situation."
— *Iraj Fooladi*
  Douglas C. Mackay Chair in Finance, School of Business Administration, Dalhousie University

"Families around the globe will enjoy reading about Victor Banks and the Atlas business—and they will gain a wealth of knowledge in doing so. The authors cover the many dilemmas facing a family-owned business with great clarity and depth of expertise. Readers will come away with a very realistic view of the contribution each specialist brings."
— *Barbara R. Hauser LLC*
  Independent advisor to global families and author of International Family Governance: A Guide for Families & their Advisors

"After 42 years of observing families and businesses owned by families, and having my own experience in these environments, I can recommend standing back from your situation with the support of a strong team of advisors as you chart the future. This story will help you in your deliberations for yourself, your family, and your business."
— *Bryce M. Hunter*
  Chairman, Hunters

"Do not do another thing about succession planning until you have read this book. *On the Shoulders of Atlas* is an easy-to-read guide for family business owners who want to take their business past their ownership and to the next stage. The results will be happy families who are both wealthy and wise."
— *Jacoline Loewen*
  Family business private equity expert, Loewen & Partners

"The example of Victor Banks and Atlas Plastics may be fiction, but the book reveals a storyline I've seen many times as a private equity fund partner. *On the Shoulders of Atlas* provides solid financial advice for family-owned businesses. Anyone in a similar situation will benefit from the authors' insights."

— *John B. MacIntyre*
Partner, Birch Hill Equity Partners

"An excellent book on the complexities of succession planning. The content covers a wide range of useful information on tax planning, trusts, private corporations, and estate planning, and will be of great interest to accountants, lawyers, portfolio managers, bankers, wealth managers, and their clients."

— *Doug Mackay*
Former Vice Chairman, RBC Dominion Securities

"As a professional advisor to family businesses, I wholeheartedly support the collaborative approach outlined in *On the Shoulders of Atlas*. The book is a must-read for business owners concerned about their businesses and their families."

— *Luanna McGowan, BA LLB LLM*
President, The McGowan Group

"A book that every family business owner should take seriously."

— *Hank Mews*
Chairman, The Myers Automotive Group

"As an advisor to owner-managed businesses for over 45 years, I recognize that the process of business succession can be sensitive and explosive. *On the Shoulders of Atlas* clearly illustrates how a team effort can guide an owner through the process to a satisfying conclusion."

— *Bernie Nisker*
President, Bernie Nisker Inc.

"*On the Shoulders of Atlas* is an insightful look at the issues entrepreneurs face as they transition their businesses. The authors deftly touch on the practical, emotional, and financial issues surrounding succession, the sale of a business, and the process of providing for multiple family stakeholders into the future. An important read for those thinking of embarking on this process as well as for those who provide trusted advice during the process."
— *Gordon Pridham*
  Chairman, Monarch Wealth

"Having spent the bulk of my career working with successful families, I know that the most difficult challenge facing entrepreneurs is not how to build the business; it is figuring out what to do when the time comes to step back from the firm that has been their life's work. The issues the business owner must deal with are complex, emotional, and multi-dimensional. In *On the Shoulders of Atlas*, the authors demonstrate how one entrepreneur, working with a range of highly competent advisors, resolved the challenges he faced. This highly readable book is a template for how to transition a business in the right way and should be read by any business owner contemplating retirement."
— *Sandy Riley*
  President and CEO, Richardson Financial Group

"The toughest issue facing business owners is how to transition their business while at the same time ensuring that the resulting wealth enhances their family. It's great to journey with Victor, Anne, their family and their advisors in *On the Shoulders of Atlas*. The advice given is understandable and real. This is a book any Canadian family with a significant business should read to gain the confidence to act on their own situation."
— *Grant Robinson*
  Partner, BDO Canada LLP

"A must-read for any private business owner. The authors have highlighted the issues and considerations facing thousands every year."
— *Gordon Schofield*
Partner, Murphy Business Canada Inc.

"While it is necessary to take into account culture and the unique character of each family, for entrepreneurs everywhere the challenges of transition are similar. *On the Shoulders of Atlas* helps people realize there is a way of working through the complex issues that arise in trying to balance multiple systems."
— *Christian Stewart*
Managing Director, Family Legacy Asia (HK) Limited

"*On the Shoulders of Atlas* offers practical and clearly set out strategies to help advisors work more effectively with family business owners—and one another. The book is valuable to both trusted advisors and their business-owner clients."
— *Evan Thompson*
Founding Partner, Thompson, Wiley + Associates
Board member, The Family Firm Institute (Ontario Chapter)

ON THE SHOULDERS OF ATLAS

ON THE SHOULDERS OF ATLAS

A STORY ABOUT TRANSITIONING A FAMILY-OWNED BUSINESS

Susan Latremoille & Peter Creaghan
with Frank Archibald, Linda Betts, Arnie Cader, Sheila Crummey,
Tony Ianni, Steve Landau, Ron Prehogan, and Pearl Schusheim

ISBN 978-0-9781401-2-0

Library and Archives Canada Cataloguing in Publication

Latremoille, Susan, 1951-
        On the shoulders of Atlas : a story about transitioning a family-owned business / Susan Latremoille & Peter Creaghan ; with Frank Archibald . . .
[et al.].

ISBN 978-0-9781401-2-0

        1. Family-owned business enterprises—Succession. 2. Strategic planning.
I. Creaghan, Peter, 1958- II. Archibald, Frank, 1952- III. Title.

HD62.25.L38 2010   658'.045   C2010-900888-X

First Edition

The Latremoille Group
Brookfield Place, 181 Bay Street, Suite 3910
Toronto, Ontario   M5J 2N3

Printed in Canada

CONTENTS

Preface / xvii

PART I
VICTOR BANKS'S DILEMMA / 1

> **Chapter 1: Victor's Situation** / 3
> **Chapter 2: Discussion Time** / 9

PART II
SOLVING VICTOR'S DILEMMA: TAKING CARE OF THE BUSINESS / 13

> **Chapter 3: Laying the Groundwork** / 15
> Atlas Plastics: Hold or Sell? / 15
> Where Are We, and Where Do We Go from Here? / 17
> What's the Financial Picture? / 19
> Who Will Run Atlas If the Family Keeps It? / 21
>
> **Chapter 4: How Do I Sell a Company?** / 27
> Preliminaries / 27
> Getting Down to Business / 30
> The Process / 31
> Private Equity or Strategic Buyer? / 35
>
> **Chapter 5: Talking Taxes: Making a Good Deal Better** / 41
> Understanding the Tax Implications / 41
> The Estate Freeze and the Trust / 42

What Are Victor's Tax Options? / 43
Just What *Is* Wrong with the Old Trust? / 47

Chapter 6: Let's Make It Legal: Getting the Deal Done / 53
Private Equity Partner: Pros and Cons / 56
Tying Up Loose Ends / 57

**PART III
SOLVING VICTOR'S DILEMMA: TAKING CARE OF OTHER BUSINESS** / 63

**Chapter 7: My Family Is My Business; My Business
Is My Family** / 65
Defining the Business / 65
Discovery Meetings / 69
Deciding to Move Ahead Together / 70

**Chapter 8: I Invested My Life in My Business—How Do I Invest
the Proceeds?** / 77
Defining the Goals / 77
Deciding What Matters / 78
Where Do We Go from Here? / 81
Combine and Conquer / 83

Chapter 9: What Should My Estate Plan Look Like? / 87
Taking Care of Rose / 88
What to Do about Robert / 90
Planning for Victor and Anne / 92

**Chapter 10: Ensuring the Outcome: Innovative Insurance
Solutions** / 97
Getting Down to Business / 99

Epilogue / 105

Appendix A: People in Victor Banks's Story / 109
Appendix B: Financial Data: Atlas and Personal Assets / 111
Appendix C: The Banks Family Empire before and after the Private
            Equity Deal / 113
Appendix D: Asset Allocation of the Investment Portfolio / 117
Appendix E: The Insurance Solution / 119

About the Authors / 121

Index / 127

PREFACE

Welcome to the story of Victor Banks, devoted husband to Anne, caring father to Anthony, Rose, Caitlin, and Robert, and—above all—visionary entrepreneur and founder and owner of Atlas Plastics. After a lifetime of success, Victor is facing the toughest challenge of his professional life: what to do with Atlas Plastics? It's got him perplexed, stuck in his tracks. For the first time in memory, Victor Banks can't see a way forward.

Victor started from scratch forty years ago. With Anne's support at home, Victor put in eighty-hour weeks and slowly built Atlas Plastics from a small family business into a global powerhouse with sales of over $200 million, far bigger than he'd imagined possible in the early days. However, Victor's been promising himself he'll spend more time away from work, and he's promised Anne he'll spend more time travelling and enjoying life. He can't seem to find a way to make good on these promises.

Atlas Plastics is still growing rapidly, with significant expansion possibilities on the horizon. When that expansion happens (and there doesn't seem to be any real choice in the matter), the company will need major investments in new plants and equipment, bigger investments than ever before. Victor's CFO has told him that if they pursue their expansion plans, he may have to reduce his withdrawal of funds from the business for personal financial security. Anne won't be happy about that because Victor's also been promising to finally retire and reduce their dependence on the business. Now that too seems impossible.

On the family side, Victor and Anne have a whole other set of issues. They have four grown children. Three work in the business, one doesn't. All are wondering what Victor plans to do next. Will he keep the business and grow it? Will he sell it? The livelihoods and careers of the children working in the business depend on his decision. For the one who doesn't, a sale may be a chance to see some financial autonomy. Yet, Victor himself can't see clearly which way makes most sense. There seem to be many conflicting possibilities.

The transitioning of a successful business like Victor's is a complex, daunting process involving technical issues such as tax planning and financial engineering and also emotional issues and family dynamics. Though Victor has built significant wealth as he built his business, this wealth is almost entirely tied up *in* the business. His key financial decisions have revolved around whether to pay down debt or borrow more to expand. For Victor, therefore, the point of transition to the next generation is the first time he's had to deal with broader tax and financial issues.

The same will be true if he decides to sell his business. In fact, the additional "challenge" of substantial liquid wealth creates a whole new set of problems: How will he invest his money wisely? Who will he trust? How will he transfer the wealth wisely to his children? What if they blow it? And, most difficult of all, what will he do with all this new time on his hands? Make no mistake about it, transition planning is almost always wrapped up with another reality: retirement. People with "regular jobs" often look ahead to retirement with excitement and a sense of adventure. But for the typical business owner like Victor Banks, retirement almost inevitably engenders more difficult feelings. Victor wonders what *not* being in business will do to his sense of identity, purpose, and fulfillment. Few endeavours in life are more engaging and rewarding than running a successful business, and Victor wonders what he'll do with his "final chapter" if he's not involved in the business.

Business owners like Victor are typically neither trained nor prepared for transition. They don't always understand the available options and have no easy way to find this information. Their professional advisors most often feel straightjacketed into historical roles (e.g., accountant, lawyer, banker) and deal with specific issues as they come up. Rarely are they invited to contribute proactively to their clients' overall financial and family planning. Where, then, does Victor find advice? With so many areas to cover, how can he find the expertise he needs? Who will quarterback this effort? How much will it cost? How long will it take? And what will be the best outcome for him and his family?

So, while we welcome you to the story of Victor Banks and his family, we also welcome you to that of a unique group of independent advisors who come together almost seamlessly to help Victor and his family work through the issues and come up with the right solution for their future. These advisors arrive from a broad variety of different specialties—tax planning, estate planning, wealth management, life insurance, and dealing with family dynamics, to name a few—and they all work in different advisory firms with independent practices. What they share is a commitment to the whole solution, to proactive advice, and to working collaboratively—with Victor and his family and also with Victor's other advisors. These specialists know their own areas of expertise, how to work together, and how to blend their talents in support of each particular engagement. They know how to first ensure that business owners achieve clarity about what they want and then structure a deal or plan to deliver the results. They know how to implement solutions that involve many specialties that must be coordinated.

Not all businesses are as large or complex as Victor's, and not all transitions require the counsel of so many advisors. Many business owners, in fact, have trusted advisors whose experience with large, complex transactions qualifies them to provide excellent advice. When this is the case, they call one or more of us in as needed. However, many business owners are like Victor, with trusted advisors who provide solid advice on day-to-day operations but don't have the time or the experience to prepare for and follow through on a company's sale or transition. We hope you'll see how we work *with* a business owner's current advisors to achieve the optimal outcome.

We hope you'll come away from this book with a better understanding of the options available as you approach your own transition. We trust that you'll be better equipped to undertake the planning *you* need to do to ensure your own company's successful transition when the time comes.

For advisors who read this book, no matter what your area of expertise, we hope you'll see the importance of developing a relationship of trust with a network of specialists in other disciplines. It is through ongoing communication and collaboration with such a network that you can best provide the service that your clients need and want.

Susan Latremoille
First Vice President and Wealth Advisor
The Latremoille Group, Richardson GMP Limited

Peter Creaghan
Partner
Creaghan McConnell Group

PART I
Victor Banks's Dilemma

Chapter 1 - Victor's Situation

Victor's father used to say, "Our family jumped from the Iron Age to the Space Age with no stops in between." He always said it with a laugh that was part pride in his son's accomplishments and part nostalgia.

Anton Bancescu settled in small-town Ontario when he came from Europe with his wife in 1935. The Depression years were tough, and many Canadians struggled to find work to feed, clothe, and shelter their families. Anton was lucky, though. He had a trade, and he found a place that needed the kind of work he knew how to do. That's what he meant by "the Iron Age." Back home, he'd been a blacksmith and metal caster, and that was the work he did here.

When he said "the Space Age," he meant the work his son did—"with contracts from NASA, if you can believe that!" he'd say. Anton wasn't pleased when Victor changed his last name to Banks when he went to university, but he understood the advantage it might give him in business and couldn't have been more pleased with his son's success.

Victor was born in 1940, and when he was old enough, he started spending time in the shop. Anton would let him stay for hours, talking to Victor the whole time, giving step-by-step explanations of whatever he happened to be working on. Victor loved watching his father work. He liked watching him pour molten iron or bronze into casts and then watching the hot liquid solidify into nails and horseshoes, fences and gates, streetlights and lamps, doorways and window grates.

When Victor was twelve, he was big enough to help his father. He soon started suggesting ways to change the casting molds to cut the time and materials needed to prepare them. His methods decreased the cost of manufacturing the cast products and improved their quality.

His father's business grew, and he became prosperous enough to turn his one-man shop into a small foundry. He encouraged Victor to study, and Victor loved learning—he'd read anything and everything. One day in his last year of high school, while waiting his turn in the barbershop, he picked up a copy of *Time* and read an article about a new industry that had begun springing up—mostly in the United States but with some small operations in Canada—the plastic molding industry. Victor saw parallels between the work he did with his father (casting molten iron and bronze) and this new industry (casting molten plastic polymers).

That article changed his life. He sensed that plastic was the way of the future and saw where this industry could go. He wanted to be the one to take it there, so he decided to study engineering. When he graduated in 1962—with the third-highest marks in his class—he got a job with Atlas Plastics, a small plastic molding company in Toronto owned and operated by George Marchek. George was in his mid-sixties, had no children, and was beginning to have health problems. He was looking for someone to take over the reins. He liked Victor. He respected his knowledge and drive. He was particularly impressed by Victor's ability to persuade even senior people to his point of view. Victor had an opinion on everything and always backed up his opinions good-naturedly—and with solid facts.

Victor had talent, ambition, and an incredible capacity to understand the practicalities of the business. He rose quickly, and though he was still young, his grasp of the technology and vision of how it could be improved landed him the offer of a senior position in the firm.

Victor knew his reputation was as good outside the firm as within, and knew the offer of promotion meant that Marchek valued him. In other words, he knew he was in a good bargaining position. He accepted the promotion and let it be known that he wanted to buy a small equity stake in the company. Marchek couldn't have been happier. They struck a deal, and between the bank and his father, Victor raised the needed funds. He became head of the new research and development department in 1967, the year his first child, Anthony, was born.

Victor was a visionary and an innovator. He oversaw groundbreaking advances that put Atlas at the forefront of the industry. Within three years, he introduced technological changes that eventually became the industry standard and integrated manufacturing systems in a way that brought rapid and profitable results.

He worked closely with Marchek, and they developed a mutual respect and affection. Before long, Victor began to see that Marchek wasn't as sharp and energetic as when they had first met. Eventually, Marchek confided in him about his health problems. He said he needed to slow down and eventually stop altogether and wanted nothing more than to see Victor take over. By the end of 1970, Victor and Marchek agreed on terms by which Victor would buy Atlas Plastics over the next five years.

These were a busy five years in the business. When he assumed full ownership in 1975, Victor had run sales and marketing and worked for two-and-a-half years as the company's chief operating officer. In that position, he'd overseen the redesign of Atlas's plant and set a strategy for further plant expansion.

They were busy years at home, too: By 1975, Victor and his wife Anne had had three more children. Rose was born in 1969,

Caitlin in 1970, and Robert in 1974. The three oldest children are now married and work in the business. Rose's husband, Michael Redding, is a senior executive in the company. Victor tells himself, "It's not quite a dynasty, but it's a start."

When he looks back, Victor wonders how the years went by so fast. His greatest accomplishment is having transformed Atlas from a small Toronto company doing business mostly with Ontario's auto industry into a multinational corporation with 1,600 employees and a reputation as an international leader in plastic molding. Still based in Toronto, Atlas now has three operating divisions and plants in North America: the automotive plant in Mississauga, the aerospace plant near Orlando, and the consumer goods plant near Chicago. It's also developed a fairly solid European market.

Victor is proud that he's remained an innovator. For more than three decades, he's kept Atlas at the forefront of research and development, and even as the industry has become more competitive, he's managed to maintain Atlas's edge.

Now, the company needs to make further major investments to maintain that edge. It needs a plant in Eastern Europe to lower production costs for the European market. It also needs to grow the consumer products division's market share in the western US, and there may be an opportunity to acquire a major California-based competitor, which would go a long way toward solving that problem. Both courses of action require substantial capital and involve substantial risk. Victor is excited by the prospect of growing his company even more, but isn't sure he wants to undertake such big moves at his age.

As if that isn't enough to think about, Victor's accountant and close friend, Paul Stenson, is insisting he make decisions he's avoided for years. Paul's always been good with accounting and general business advice, and Victor values his counsel. But a recent meeting with Paul left Victor feeling burdened and bewildered.

That night, he told Anne about the meeting. "After we reviewed the business stuff, Paul said we should look at investments outside the business because, at our age, it's not good to have so much of our wealth tied up in the business. Then he started asking a thousand questions about what my plans are. When will I retire? Am I keeping the business or selling it? Do the kids want to stay in the business? Who'll run it when I leave? What if they run it into the ground? And what if one wants to cash out? How would it affect the company's viability?

"Anyway, then Paul asked if I've thought about tax on death. He said it could be a big problem if I keep the company and the kids end up with it."

Paul had also reminded Victor about the estate freeze he had done fifteen years ago and about setting up the trust. "He said we need a new arrangement on that because in six more years, there's some kind of deemed disposition, and that could mean a gigantic tax bill."

Paul had mentioned getting private equity people to put up capital and become financial partners so that some of Atlas's value could be turned to cash and Victor could avoid having everything tied up in the business. This idea was unsettling to Victor because Atlas wouldn't be a family company anymore.

"Anne, we rely on Paul. He's given us solid, practical advice year after year. I know we've talked about all this before, but I guess I was too busy running the business for it to sink in. It always seemed so far in the future. Now here we are. He's asking questions I can't really answer and telling me it's important that I come up with the answers soon. But to tell you the truth, I think he really doesn't know any better than I do about exactly what we should do. I think he's right that we need more planning, but I think it's a more complex situation than he's dealt with before. He suggested we get some help to figure these things out."

Anne had already told Victor what she thought he should do, though she wasn't convinced he'd do it. She wondered why Victor was even considering further expansion. As far as she was concerned, Victor had worked hard enough. He'd built a successful business and provided a great lifestyle for his family. She thought it was time for them to cash out and enjoy life while they were both still active and able.

The long-range plan when they had gotten married had been to have a family and for Victor to work hard, build the business, and retire by sixty-five so they could enjoy a nice, long retirement together. What Anne hadn't told him was that she was feeling a bit lonely. The children were adults now, and Victor was still putting in long days at work. Anne wanted to spend more time together. She wanted to travel more, see the world, and spend more time at the cottage.

Anne kept quiet, though. Victor was clearly upset. Instead, she said, "You know how the whole family comes to the cottage for Canada Day weekend? That's just a few weeks away. Why don't we make it into a family meeting where we can straighten some of these things out?"

"That's a great idea, Anne."

Chapter 2 - Discussion Time

On the Friday morning of the Canada Day weekend, Victor and Anne were up early. In their family, it had always been a four-day weekend, and there was lots to do before the rest of the family arrived. Victor stood on the dock. The morning was clear and quiet—a perfect day, Victor thought, to sort out the things he needed to figure out. But by Monday night, he couldn't believe how many crosscurrents had emerged since lunchtime on Friday.

As they sat in their Muskoka chairs on the dock that evening, after most of the family had headed back to the city, Victor and Anne discussed the weekend's events and traumas.

"I can't believe Michael assumes he'll be the one to take over the business when I step down. To say no one else in the family has his experience or management ability or vision about the business is quite bold. I wish I could say he's wrong, but he's not. He's really pushing for the European plant and the US acquisition, and I have to admit he's done his homework. But still, to dismiss Anthony like that when Anthony's sitting right in front of him!"

"Victor, take a minute and think back over the years. You and I both know Michael's always been out for himself. Something about him just doesn't sit right with me."

"I know what you mean, but being out for yourself isn't a bad thing in business. If I hadn't had my own best interests in mind, if I hadn't taken advantage of every situation, I never could have built Atlas into the company it is today."

"I'm sure that's true, but there's taking advantage of situations and then there's taking advantage of people."

"Right. The whole time Michael was blowing his own horn, I was thinking of Chris Carter. He's every bit as capable of running the company as Michael is, and he's a lot easier to get along with. A real self-starter. He's got good experience in lots of different areas of the company, and he's done a great job as chief operating officer. A few years as CFO, and he might even make a stronger leader than Michael. And he's dedicated to Atlas. Michael just figures I'd never let the decision-making pass out of family hands."

Anne thought about this a minute. "But can you be sure Michael's 'family hands' will stay in the family? Just look how he treats Rose sometimes."

"I wish Anthony could run the company, but he simply doesn't have what it takes. He does do a damn good job of managing the plants, though. The fact is, he's a great lieutenant, but he'll never be a general."

Then Victor mentioned their grandson, Stephen. "Now there's someone who could run my company some day. What a kid! MIT at seventeen. He's been top of his class every year. And he's loved working at Atlas all those summers since he was fifteen."

"Victor, what did you think of Robert's proposal?" Anne asks.

"That wasn't a proposal, Anne—it was a pipe dream. Did you see the eyes rolling while he was talking?"

"But it's the first time he's expressed any interest in working for the company. It might be good for him. It'd give him something to do."

"Anne, you don't employ a person to give him something to do. You pay a person because he can do something you need done. He's thirty-five, and as far as I can see, he can't do anything Atlas needs."

Victor used to wonder how Robert managed to maintain his lifestyle. He got occasional gigs in the film business, but how much could that bring in? He had a nice apartment and drove a late-model German car, and from the way he talked, it sounded like he was a regular at some of Vancouver's most expensive restaurants. Then Paul Stenson took Victor aside one day and asked, "Do you realize how much money Anne is giving Robert?" So that was it. Anne was taking care of her pet.

Anne wanted to change gears, so she decided to fill Victor in on some gossip. "Well, at least one piece of exciting news came out this weekend. I'm not really supposed to let you know for two more weeks, because she's not at the three-month mark yet, but Caitlin's pregnant!"

Immediately, Victor wondered what this meant for the business. "She's waited so long and tried so hard to get pregnant. Will she stay home with the baby? At least we've got a second-in-command to run human resources if she leaves."

"Oh, Victor. Honestly—leave Atlas out of your thoughts for one minute. It's another grandbaby!"

One thing was clear from the weekend's discussions: None of the kids seemed anxious to sell the company. Victor still wasn't sure *he* wanted to sell. Anne was right—the plan had been for him to retire at sixty-five. The weekend hadn't brought him any closer to a decision about who would take over if he decided not to sell.

Victor came out of his reverie, noticing Anthony coming up the dock with a pot of coffee. All he could think was that the last thing he needed right then was a showdown about the rights of the firstborn.

"Hey, Dad. I thought you might want some more coffee," Anthony said.

"Sure. Top me up."

After filling Victor's cup, Anthony set the pot on the deck and sat in an empty chair.

"Dad, I've been thinking. I think I have something important to contribute, and I'm asking you, not just as a colleague, but also as a son, to seriously consider what I'm about to say. I know you've always relied on yourself to make business decisions, but you always bring in the best people to make sure you have the right information first. The decisions you're making now aren't just about the business—they're about the family, too. But what's happened this weekend, with all the disagreements and discussions, tells me this won't get solved alone."

Victor was listening with great attention.

"I think there *is* a solution," Anthony continued. "I know you know Artie Granger, who used to run Mayfair Markets, but I bet you don't know he went through what you're going through three years ago. I golf with his son Jack, and Jack told me how their family did it. They called in people who help business owners and their families make clear decisions when a transition is about to happen. Call Artie and talk to him about the people who helped him out. Will you do that, Dad?"

Surprised that Anthony was giving him advice, Victor didn't answer right away. Then he remembered that Paul Stenson had said something similar.

"I'll call Artie Granger tomorrow morning. Thanks, son. I'm glad you decided to tell me how you feel."

PART II

Solving Victor's Dilemma: Taking Care of the Business

Chapter 3 - Laying the Groundwork

by Ron Prehogan
President, Equitas Consultants Inc.

Atlas Plastics: Hold or Sell?

The first time I met Victor Banks was over lunch at the Bloor Street Diner. Victor chose the diner because it was near his office, and he loved the steak frites.

A client of mine, Artie Granger, had encouraged Victor to have a meeting with me—what I call the chemistry meeting or the get-to-know-you meeting. Victor wanted a clearer picture of what I do, what the process involves, and how long it takes. But he also wanted a feeling for who I was. Was I someone he could work with? I wanted the same sense about him, because the work we do at Equitas requires mutual trust and respect between clients and ourselves.

Though he didn't go into much detail, Victor told me about the weekend at the cottage. He said he'd hoped to make some important decisions about his business and his future involvement in it, but many issues came up that made this difficult.

From talking to Artie Granger, Victor knew that Equitas focuses on two objectives:

1. Helping business owners gain clarity about succession planning, and
2. Helping them implement the plan.

I further clarified that succession planning is really an information-gathering and assessment process. "First, we meet with you and your wife, then individually with your children who work in the business, and then with other key people in the business. We ask them to be candid about their thoughts and feelings about the business, other family members, and their business associates, who can also be family. Then we have group meetings with all these people to discuss the issues that surface in the individual meetings."

Victor grunted. "Jeez, that sounds like it could take forever. I need to make these decisions now."

"It can take a long time—from weeks to months, depending on people's availability and candor. But to make the best decisions, you need the best information, and this is how we get it—by gaining people's respect and trust and having them tell us what's on their minds."

"Why would they tell you things they might not want me to hear?" he asked.

"If we end up working together, we won't be acting as *your* agent exclusively. Rather, the business and the family would be our clients, and we'd be acting in everyone's interests. Nothing anyone says gets attributed unless the person wants it that way. This lets people feel comfortable speaking to us about anything on their minds: what they like about the business, what they think should be changed, who they work well with, who they don't, and why."

Victor seemed a bit taken aback that we wouldn't be answerable to him, but then realized it made sense.

As we spoke, one thing became clear: A decision whether to sell had *not* been made. To come to a final and reasoned decision about the future of his company—and family—Victor needed to explore both options fully and run two different *what-if* scenarios simultaneously.

In a situation such as this, I get the client to think through a few questions:

- *What if I sell the business?*
- *What's it worth?*
- *How should the sale be structured?*
- *What are the tax ramifications? How do I deal with them?*
- *What do I do with the proceeds?*
- *What about my kids—what's fair to them?*
- *If I keep the business in the family, who will run it? Who will oversee the way that person operates?*
- *How can I ensure responsible stewardship after I die?*

These were the same questions on Victor's mind, questions he would have to answer.

All in all, that first meeting went well. Victor Banks and Equitas were beginning a long journey toward gaining clarity on how to transition Atlas Plastics. As I told Victor when we first met, transitioning a business isn't an event—it's a process.

Where Are We, and Where Do We Go from Here?

We had four meetings with Victor and Anne. The purpose was straightforward: to get them to talk about where they saw themselves at present and agree on where they wanted to go. They discussed how they felt about their lifestyle, their financial situation, family issues they were facing, and the legacy they wanted to leave.

Anne had some critically important insights. Like many wives, she was the emotional glue of the family. It was Anne who knew that Michael and Rose might be having marital difficulties and that Caitlin was pregnant. It was Anne who told Victor how disenfranchised Anthony felt. She also helped me understand things about Victor that I'd otherwise never have learned.

At one point, she said, "When Victor and I first married, we had a dream for how our life would be. I knew I'd be home with the children and that Victor would put most of his energy into the business. His drive and focus were things I loved about him—they were, and are, part of him. I always had faith in his ability and knew what support he needed from me. In many ways, it's been a great life. I put as much energy into raising the kids as he put into the business, and I don't regret a day of it.

"But Victor was going to retire by sixty-five. Then we were going to make up for lost time . . . do a lot of travelling . . . spend long, lazy summer months at the cottage and have the kids and grandkids come up whenever they could. Well, now he's sixty-nine and still working every day. I have to tell you: What I *do* regret is that that part of the dream hasn't come true."

Victor got a little testy. "Do I have to defend myself for making a success of Atlas? The company still needs me."

"Yes, Victor, I know, I know. But I need you, too."

This was a catalytic moment. I said, "Anne's just revealed how she feels. There's no need to get onto a blame-and-defend track. How about using this as an opportunity to recast your dream, to decide what your new dream will be?"

They both got it: Victor cooled down—he even said he knew Anne deserved more from him. Anne said she'd welcome having a common vision rather than simply wondering from day to day, week to week, and month to month what their future would be.

Anne was clear that she wanted Victor to sell the business and for them to live on the proceeds, splitting their estate equally among the children when they died. Victor was ambivalent: Should he marshal on with the business and grow it to the next level, pass the reins on but keep the business in the family, or, as Anne suggested, sell the business altogether? Victor seemed to be leaning toward option number two—passing on the reins, but keeping the business in the family.

Victor and Anne spoke candidly about their children. They discussed the troublesome information that had come out over the weekend at the cottage. In one meeting, Victor told Anne that he knew she'd been subsidizing Robert's lifestyle for years. Anne's response was that someone had to look after him.

Though they had their moments of conflict, they were fairly in sync in their assessment of their children, both personally and in terms of their potential contribution to the business. They agreed that none of their children was a serious contender to run the company, and both were concerned about Robert. Though neither was completely comfortable with Rose's husband Michael, both thought he was capable, and they considered Chris Carter a competent steward but not a visionary.

When our fourth meeting ended, Victor and Anne had indeed reframed their dream and agreed on a mutually satisfying future together. It included a common vision of their future lifestyle, their desire to leave a legacy to their children (though the exact shape of that legacy wasn't fully formulated), and an outline of their philanthropic goals. It also underscored the fact that Victor needed to convert at least part of his equity in Atlas into cash to have liquid funds to support their plans.

The foundation piece was that Victor would disengage from Atlas in two years, and then their original retirement plans would kick in—albeit six years late!

What's the Financial Picture?

The success of this part of the process depends on both spouses being completely engaged, and Victor and Anne certainly were. One basic objective achieved in those meetings was figuring out what their future together should look like.

Once they sketched that out, the question arose of how to fund their retirement years. Victor's accountant, Paul Stenson, joined us to help us understand Victor and Anne's current financial situation and annual financial requirements once Victor left Atlas. (See Appendix B for a table of the Banks family's assets.)

The discussion began straightforwardly. Anne didn't want to change their lifestyle. "I certainly want to live out the rest of my life as comfortably as I've lived the past forty years, and Victor surely deserves to do the same. After all, he's the one who built Atlas, and he should reap the rewards of his success."

So it was agreed that they planned to maintain their current lifestyle in retirement. But determining the best way to fund their retirement years and looking at the bigger financial picture after Victor's retirement turned out to be different matters. There were far more questions than answers, starting with questions about the estate freeze that had been done fifteen years earlier and the trust that had been established at the time.

For instance, Victor remembered that the freeze had been done for tax purposes but only vaguely recollected the details. In this, Victor is like many family business owners—his real focus is on his business, and his personal financial planning took a back seat to that.

Paul reminded him that it was a basic freeze involving a discretionary trust with the children as beneficiaries and Victor and Anne as trustees. Victor and Anne had updated their wills at the same time, simple wills in which each left everything to the other.

Victor interrupted Paul as he was talking about the freeze. He'd completely lost sight of the fact that only his children would benefit from the company's growth in value over the past fifteen years.

"Wait a minute—go over that again. If I die tomorrow, Anne will inherit only a small part of the company's total value? And the kids will get the rest?"

This got us into a discussion of the trust and its tax implications, which got us into a broader discussion of Atlas's overall financial picture, which inevitably got us into a discussion of the financial and tax consequences of the alternative courses of action Victor was considering—i.e., to keep and expand the business or to sell it altogether. We were still trying to get a handle on how to fund the retirement years.

At one point, Victor turned to me and said, "Artie Granger told me about some of the people you recommended when he was figuring out this whole thing for himself. He liked how they worked with his own advisors to put the whole picture in focus. I think it's time we called on some of them."

After some discussion with Paul Stenson, Atlas CFO Chris Carter, and Victor's lawyer, Jonathan Hill, we decided Victor and his people should have a separate round of discovery meetings about finances. In the following chapters, you'll meet the people who worked with Victor and his advisors to get the answers he needed. Each will talk about his or her part in Victor's story. For now, though, let's turn back to the work Equitas did.

Who Will Run Atlas If the Family Keeps It?

With Victor and Anne's personal issues resolved and their new dream sketched out, it was time to talk to the people who made Atlas work, day in and day out. While the finance meetings were going on, my partner, Ken Andrews, and I met individually with Victor, his three children and son-in-law who worked in the business, and some key senior management personnel.

We made it clear that they could say whatever they wanted, that nothing was off limits, and that we'd protect their privacy when dealing with sensitive issues so that nothing they said would come back to sting them. These individual meetings went well. The participants openly shared their views about the company and its future, and the potential roles they saw for themselves and others once Victor stepped down.

Our meeting with Victor confirmed that his desire to keep the business in the family was largely fuelled by the potential he saw in his grandson, Stephen, whom he could easily imagine running the company one day. However, Victor was fully aware that this was at least a decade or two away, so deciding on the next CEO was critical. We explored all possibilities and discussed his views on each potential successor.

After these meetings, we brought everyone together to summarize what we'd heard and the key issues that had emerged. More importantly, we needed to discuss the leadership transition process if the business were to remain in the family. Let's look in on that meeting.

Imagine a corporate boardroom, forty-three stories up. On one side of a table, with their backs to the windows, sit Victor, Anthony, Rose, Caitlin, Michael Redding, Paul Stenson, and Chris Carter. They face a whiteboard on the other side of the table. Standing just to the left of the whiteboard is Ken Andrews, and I am sitting to the right.

Ken opens the meeting. "I want to remind you that we're here to look at certain issues together and resolve these issues as a group if we can. This isn't about who said what, and it's not about blame. It's about figuring out what Atlas looks like when Victor is no longer CEO, and it's about making Atlas even stronger than it already is."

Everyone agrees that this is what they're there for, so the meeting gets under way. Ken writes one word on the board and underlines it: <u>Victor</u>. Beneath Victor's name, he writes three words: *autocratic, controlling, micro-managing*.

In our meeting with Anthony, he'd said that he thought he deserved more decision-making responsibility. Others echoed his complaint.

After writing this, Ken says, "Victor, these are words that came up in our individual meetings when different people were talking about you, and they're not surprising descriptions. After all, you had the vision of what Atlas could be, and your decision-making built it into the company it is today. What we're talking about today is transition, so I won't ask you what you think of this description; I will ask you what you think of it as a description of a man who's about to let go of the reins of a $250-million-dollar company."

They say the person who gets to ask the questions holds the power. By framing the question the way he did, by taking the personal element out of it, Ken could focus everyone's attention—including Victor's—on the underlying *common* problem: How can people who have never been allowed to exercise substantial decision-making authority be expected to run a company of this size?

With Ken facilitating the meeting and keeping everyone properly focused, they homed in on issues as they related to the company's health, even when they had initially been raised in the individual meetings as interpersonal problems.

For instance, many people remarked about Michael's brusqueness. Ken wrote three words under Michael's name on the whiteboard: *bulldozer, confrontational, insensitive.* Michael seemed to have been oblivious to his effect on people. Learning about it made him see the liability it was, not only for him personally but also for Atlas's success if he was going to play a significant part in its future, as he said he really wanted to do.

This meeting laid the necessary groundwork for many more over the following months, meetings delving into issues such as whether to sell the business or keep it in the family, who would succeed Victor if the business were to remain in the family, and what structures and processes were needed for a successful transition. Our meetings ran in parallel with Tony Ianni's finance meetings (the subject of the next chapter), and the group answered these important questions with input from Tony and his people.

It was agreed that if Atlas were to survive and thrive as a multigenerational company, personal issues needed to be separated from business planning issues, and ownership issues from management issues. We suggested that the group do two things:

1. Set up an advisory board to oversee the company's operations. I recommended the board include an independent director. I put Victor in touch with Arnie Cader, who has worked as an independent director and trustee for some of Canada's leading business families.

2. Establish a family council to keep the family informed about the business and provide appropriate ownership input from the family to the board as required.

Victor's immediate concern was who would run the company as he transitioned out. Ken and I saw four potential options for CEO: Michael Redding, Chris Carter, Michael and Chris as co-CEOs, and a professional manager hired from the outside.

Our discussions about succession inevitably led to the question of appropriate compensation. We stressed the difference between ownership and management. From a business management perspective, compensation should be based on what a job is worth to the company and what a particular person is worth in that job.

Victor definitely got it when Ken said, "In other words, people should get paid for what they can do for Atlas, not for their last name. If you want to provide more for your children, you should figure out a way to do it outside the business."

We suggested Atlas implement a compensation package and a strategic planning and leadership development program for key management personnel. The group liked this idea and engaged Equitas in the next stage of the process: designing and implementing the program.

Ken and I were pleased with our work in laying the groundwork for a successful leadership transition. We've been called family business advisors, navigators, facilitators, and process consultants. Knowing we helped Victor through one of his career's toughest challenges is all that matters to us.

DIRECTOR'S SUMMARY *by* Arnie Cader

Ron suggested Victor set up an advisory board for Atlas and that it should include an independent director. I don't know whether Victor interviewed others for that position, but he and I met several times. He liked my experience on boards of private family companies and asked me to be the independent advisor/director. My comments as director and trustee are found throughout this book.

Over the next two months, as discussions progressed about reorganizing Atlas, Victor and Anne gave serious thought to their estate plan. They invited me to become a trustee of the trust he had established fifteen years ago and of a new trust soon to be established.

Victor was about to move from controlling a wholly owned, private company where he called the shots to something more complex—either selling it outright or selling a partial interest. Other family members might be on the advisory board, and non-family members might be involved. If a private equity investor bought an interest in Atlas, he or she would want representation on a formal board of directors. This was a watershed moment because it was time to change to a more corporate structure—not necessarily as formal as a public company structure, but certainly more participatory and formal than it had been.

Why is having an independent director on the board beneficial? Ron and Ken explained to Victor that a properly constituted board could provide needed oversight, advice, and direction for the company's operations and succession issues. Victor had no idea how to work with a board, so part of my responsibility was to explain how a board functions and what his role as chairman would be and to help him decide who should sit on the board.

Being independent meant I could offer objective advice about what would be good or bad for the business and how his family members might be involved. Having acted as an independent director on several private and public company boards during the last thirty years, I assured Victor I'd bring my energy and experience to Atlas and its operations and would spend whatever time was required to help him, the company, and his family during and after the transition.

Chapter 4 - How Do I Sell a Company?

by Tony Ianni
President, Transaction Advisory Services
Ernst & Young and Orenda Corporate Finance Inc.

Preliminaries

My first impression of Victor Banks was positive. We met in his office with Victor and Ron Prehogan, who had arranged the meeting at Victor's request. Victor was basically interviewing me to see if he wanted to engage my firm to resolve his corporate finance issues.

One of Victor's issues was his need to realize at least part of the equity he'd built in his company. Victor and Anne wanted to ensure they could maintain their lifestyle, ensure a legacy for their children, and carry out their philanthropic objectives. The corporate finance issues stemmed from the different ways Victor could do that. The available options included:

- *Recapitalizing/refinancing the business while maintaining 100 percent ownership,*
- *Selling the business outright, and*
- *Selling only a partial interest in the business.*

Victor talked at a fairly high level, describing his business, some of his key people, and the situation he faced at that moment, but he didn't provide many details. He talked about annual sales, where Atlas had its operations, and which family members were in the business. I didn't expect him to get much more specific than that, so I kept at a high level too, talking generally about the types of transactions we do, what the process looks like, and how we structure an engagement.

The main focus for the initial meeting was to see if we could gel. He wanted to know if he could trust me with his baby, and I wanted a feel for him and whether a sale or refinancing of his company, either in whole or in part, was a viable engagement for my firm.

I know Victor interviewed others for this role, so I can only surmise he also formed a positive opinion in that meeting, because days later, he called to say he wanted to talk more in-depth about his situation and potential solutions.

Our second meeting was just us, in Victor's office. I had barely sat down when he pushed a piece of paper across the table.

"I made sure we sent you the information you asked for, so my questions are on this sheet. Before we go through them, you should know I've thought a lot about the three options we discussed for getting cash out of the business, and, given the amount of money I think I need and the required future capital investment Atlas requires, I think it makes sense to sell some equity."

Victor was organized, and his questions were what you would expect someone in his position to want to know. There were two sets of questions:

Outright Sale
- *Can I sell Atlas? For how much?*
- *Who are the potential buyers?*
- *What are the steps in the process?*
- *How long will it take?*

Partial Sale—Private Equity
- *If I sell 47 percent of Atlas, what am I likely to get for it?*
- *Who are the private equity people who would be interested?*

- *What are the steps in that process?*
- *How long will it take?*

In both cases, he wanted to know what my fee would be. I went over the fee arrangement, which is fairly standard: a work fee paid monthly for the first several months and then a success fee, which is a percentage of the transaction value when and if a transaction takes place. If there *is* a transaction at the end of the process, the work fee is credited against the success fee.

The average duration of the process is about eight months. I told Victor that my team would have to complete our due diligence about Atlas before I could answer some of his other questions in detail and with confidence. From the little I knew of Victor so far, he didn't seem given to understatement, but when I told him that, based on the information he'd given me, an outright sale of his business should bring him about $250 million (less debt), he was taken aback.

Almost immediately, he asked, "What about a partial sale?"

That's where the conversation got a little tricky. I had to tell him that sale of a bit less than half his business wouldn't mean $150 million; it'd mean more like between $125 and $140. This is because private equity people generally prefer a control position in a company and pay a premium for that control. If you're offering only a minority position, two things happen:

1. You lose the control premium, and
2. You narrow the field of interested private equity players.

It's generally wiser to retain about 60 or 65 percent of your business if you're selling a minority interest.

Victor didn't want to hear that. "Fifty-three percent gives me control, and control is what I'm thinking about with this private equity scenario. So why wouldn't I sell 47 percent? Obviously, I'd get more money for more of the business."

"You're right," I said. "You would. But think about this: What happens if Atlas needs to raise capital a year or two down the line—say, $30 million for the European plant? Some of it may have to come in equity. Let's say you get $20 million in debt, so there's still $10 million in equity to raise, and let's say that, for whatever reason, you can't come up with your $5 million and your private equity partner ponies up for the entire amount. What happens? Suddenly, your equity position gets whittled down to under 50 percent, and you no longer control Atlas."

"Yeah," Victor said, "but who knows whether we'll do a project like that, and even if we do, why would you assume I couldn't come up with the $5 million?"

"In our experience, staying a bit on the conservative side has worked out better more often than not. If a controlling interest is a top priority, this approach is like an insurance policy that pays off big-time in the event of unforeseen complications."

"Let's leave it for now. I'll have to think about it."

Getting Down to Business

Soon after that meeting, we signed a letter of engagement and my people and I began working on Victor's behalf toward a transaction. I was glad to hear Victor say he wanted Anne involved in the process. When you get right down to decision-making time, it's most often a family decision, and the spouse's input is usually influential.

Anne was impressive. She didn't have a thorough knowledge of the business but certainly had a good picture of it, painted in broad strokes. Like Victor, she was direct—not strident, just firm and clear. The first time she joined us, she told me, "Victor certainly knows, and you should know too, that I think he should sell Atlas. But he's explained this process, and I'm willing to keep an open mind as it unfolds, as long as he honours our agreement—in two years, he's out of day-to-day involvement in Atlas's operations."

We started putting the pieces in place to position Atlas to potential buyers. We needed to know everything about Atlas and its operations. Victor already knew we'd need his management team's cooperation to get the information we needed.

Business owners can be wary about this part of the process because often they haven't told their key people that they're considering a sale. But Victor's key people were mostly family members who knew what was going on, so he wasn't concerned about them bolting or blabbing. Chris Carter, who knew about the potential sale, also was aware that Victor was working with his lawyer, Jonathan Hill, to draft an employment agreement that would not only guarantee him a handsome payout in the event of a transaction but also ensure his confidentiality regarding the process.

The management team was extremely open and helpful—more so than we expected, given some of the personal dynamics Ron and Ken had told us about. It's always good to be aware of any underlying problems, because the last thing you want when putting a deal together is surprises. With that knowledge in hand, we were now well prepared to position Atlas to potential buyers.

The Process

Victor is very hands-on and wanted to understand and be involved in everything we were doing. It was easy to get him to appreciate the difference between how a private equity player would look at the business and how someone interested in acquiring the business outright would look at it. We call the latter type strategic buyers—or, simply, strategics—because their interest in a business is part of a larger strategy for their own businesses. Strategics tend to be suppliers, customers, or competitors, so, one way or another, they're in the seller's space, which has its own problems.

It took Victor a while to get comfortable with the idea that suppliers, customers, or competitors would be looking at Atlas's financial performance. He was emotional about it, afraid that things would change fast if word got out that his business was up for sale: Would sales dry up? Would suppliers contract his credit terms? Would competitors get an edge?

This isn't an uncommon reaction, and Victor wanted to know who we identified as strategics and to approve contact with each of them. Victor vetoed one strategic buyer as soon as he heard the name. "That guy's bad news. I wouldn't want any of my people working for him."

The private equity side was different. These people didn't operate in Victor's space, and he didn't feel threatened by them. He wanted to know how we find potential private equity investors. What we do is identify investors who have an interest, have a track record in the appropriate industry segment, and would be a fit with the company culture. We had *carte blanche* to contact those we thought were a good fit.

Victor's involvement was both good and bad—good because it's helpful when clients are thoroughly invested in the process and forthcoming with information, but bad if they focus so much on what we're doing that their companies' performance starts to slip.

So, at one point, I had to say, "Listen, Victor, there's something you need to understand. Part of what we're doing here is preparing a forecast of Atlas's performance. Those are the numbers that potential buyers will see. The worst thing when we come down to the wire with a bidder is a surprise in the numbers. So let's make a deal here—our job will be to take care of everything that needs to happen to maximize value for you in whatever transaction takes place. Your job is to continue running Atlas so that the company's results match the forecast."

"Come on, you're not telling me that a buyer will be disappointed if Atlas knocks the socks off the forecast on the upside, are you?"

"Yes, that's exactly what I'm telling you. Coming in off-forecast raises the spectre of volatility. The buyer thinks, 'These guys can't forecast accurately. That means there's more volatility in the business than their numbers show, which means there's more risk.' And when a buyer starts thinking that way, it means the bid won't be a nice clean one. It won't be 'We like the business; we're willing to offer $300 million for it.' It'll be something like 'We like the business, but we're worried about volatility; we're willing to give you $250 million up front, with $50 million over three years, contingent on hitting certain targets.'"

Needless to say, Victor suddenly saw the wisdom in keeping his hands on the wheel.

We produced three marketing documents to get started:

1. A teaser,
2. A confidentiality agreement (CA), and
3. Two versions of a confidential information memorandum (CIM).

These documents go out to the potential buyers we identify, both to the private equity investors and the strategics. With their inside knowledge of the business and the family, Ron and Ken helped guide us in creating these materials.

By this time, Victor had decided how much of Atlas he would offer to private equity investors. He decided to go with a more conservative number than initially planned—35 percent, rather than 47 percent. He understood that although the steps in the process would be pretty much the same for the private equity people and the strategics, the particular information they'd see would be different.

"Private equity people are really financial engineers," I told him. "They're interested in structure, specifically financial structure. You have engineers to design and build your plants so they work how you want them to work. Well, these people look at a company the same way: Does it have the right management and capital structure and the right operations to produce the right financial results for us in the right amount of time—usually five to seven years? Strategics are different because they tend to look at a company from the perspective of how it fits with their own business."

To create the two different confidential information memoranda (one for the strategics and one for the private equity people), we needed an experienced tax advisor to work out the most tax-efficient structure to present to the strategics and the most tax-efficient structure to present to the private equity people. Victor interviewed several tax advisors and chose Steve Landau and Pearl Schusheim from our firm; you'll read more about the tax considerations in the next chapter.

Like many business owners, Victor was conservative in his use of debt, but he understood why private equity people like to see more debt in the capital structure: They're interested in return on equity, and the more debt there is, the higher the return on equity. So we worked out how much debt Victor could tolerate and based our CIM to the private equity investors on that. We wanted to make sure we put the same debt structure out to all the private equity people and that they all priced their bids off that.

"We want an apples-to-apples scenario when the bids come in," I told Victor. "We don't want Firm A coming in with one debt structure and bidding one amount, and then Firm B coming in with a completely different debt structure and bidding a completely different amount."

Victor quickly recognized that by adding additional debt to the balance sheet, he could re-leverage his own equity position in the company alongside that of the private equity investor. As a result, he could extract more money from the business than just the purchase price being offered by the private equity investor.

With our due diligence completed, and with Victor's approval of all the marketing documents we created, the actual sale process began. We sent the teaser—a one-pager that presents high-level information about the offer but doesn't identify the company—to the strategic buyers we'd identified. It generally takes strategics longer to maneuver through the process, so we generally send materials to them first and send materials to private equity people later.

Those interested in learning more signed the CA, which requires potential buyers to keep any information they get about the company confidential and prevents them from soliciting employees from the company. Victor was skeptical about whether people would actually honour their obligations under the CA, so he was relieved to hear that word only gets out about a deal in a small number of cases, and when it does, it's usually at the eleventh hour.

Once potential buyers sign a CA, we send them a copy of the CIM. A CIM is a much more detailed document. In this case, it identified Atlas as the seller, positioned the reason for selling (i.e., Victor's eventual retirement from the company), and provided detailed financial information about the company—all the information a buyer would need to put together a bid in the form of an expression of interest (EOI) in Atlas. An EOI is a simple two- to three-page document indicating a party's interest in the business, how much it's interested in acquiring, and how much it's willing to pay.

Private Equity or Strategic Buyer?

When the EOIs came in, there were eight from strategic buyers and five from private equity buyers. My team and I analyzed all the bids, then went over them with Victor.

He was astonished by the marked differences between them. "I could drive a Mack truck through the gap between their bids, and I don't mean from different bidders—I mean between the range of prices on any one of these things. Look at this one—this guy's saying somewhere between $220 and $280 million!"

"That's how this stage of the process goes," I said. "It's our first chance to weed out the tire-kickers and decide who to invite to walk further down the path to a transaction."

In the end, we invited four strategics and three private equity bidders to proceed. The next step would permit each interested bidder to interact face-to-face with the leadership team, the heads of all the functional areas of the company, in a presentation led by Michael Redding. These meetings would be the bidders' opportunity to do more due diligence. The private equity people, in particular, would want to assess management's strengths and weaknesses.

Victor had told us early on that he liked the idea of Michael Redding and Chris Carter as co-CEOs. We pointed out that having co-CEOs would likely raise red flags for private equity investors—they'd assume that Michael held the position because of his family status, not ability. They might then interpret this structure as inefficient and become wary. Victor saw the logic in this, and after he went back to the group in the business meetings with Ron and Ken, they decided Michael was the best candidate. The meetings with bidders would be most effective if we positioned Michael as CEO and Chris as CFO, as a dynamic combination of strategic vision and financial rigour, which, in fact, was exactly what they were.

"Remember, we're selling the future, not the past," we told Victor and his team. We helped Michael and Chris build a presentation that showcased the business and their particular talents, then put them through a dry run. When they were ready, we went to the strategics first, starting with the least logical buyer. This way, Michael and Chris could run through their presentation and fine-tune it as they moved to increasingly high-stakes situations.

In each case, we told the prospective buyer what we liked about the EOI and pointed out specific things to consider more closely. Basically, we gave directions for tightening up the bid if the buyer decided to come back to us with a letter of intent (LOI). An LOI is usually an 8- to 12-page document in which a buyer provides much more detail about a bid; it represents a very serious interest on the buyer's part.

Victor needed to retain a law firm experienced in sale transactions. His existing lawyer, Jonathan Hill, had been helpful over the years with real estate, contractual, and employment law issues and had been effective in organizing Atlas's documents for the due-diligence process, but he didn't handle significant sale transactions. We emphasized that completing a sale transaction was intensive from a legal perspective. Victor needed an experienced lawyer not only to protect himself and his interests but also to ensure everyone focused on the real issues. An experienced transaction lawyer could better anticipate issues and help provide solutions.

We gave Victor the names of several lawyers, and he selected Frank Archibald of McMillan LLP. Frank was involved from this time on, and his involvement is summarized in Chapter 6.

Two strategics and two private equity investors submitted LOIs. My team, including Steve Landau and Pearl Schusheim, analyzed the LOIs. Frank provided his input, and then we presented the LOIs to Victor. This was pretty much the moment of truth, albeit a moment that lasted several days as Victor and Anne considered the offers. They asked Arnie Cader's advice and conferred with their children.

In many ways, the easiest decision would be to go with a strategic buyer. That way, Victor would cash in completely on all the equity he'd built up in Atlas and could live out his days with no worries about money or his company. Taking on a private equity partner would mean that Victor could maintain a controlling interest in Atlas, but it'd also mean lots of change and stress. Victor was used to doing things his own way, but now there would be a formal board of directors. The equity partner would have representation on the board, and Victor would have to attend board meetings. There would be formal job descriptions and formal earnings forecasts, and coming in on target would be important. The equity partner would insist on formal budgets; would play a key role in determining compensation, including bonuses; and might want to discontinue dividend payments.

Nonetheless, Victor decided to go to the next step with one private equity investor. This included undergoing intense negotiations aimed at increasing the investor's bid and securing terms and conditions favourable to Victor. Victor had to grant a period of exclusivity to the private equity investor during which it could do more thorough due diligence; he couldn't negotiate with any other interested party at this time. Only at this stage did Victor divulge the terms of his NASA contracts—contracts that put Atlas ahead of its competitors in the aerospace division.

In the end, the negotiations produced a deal with which Victor was happy, and how he decided on the structure of that deal is the topic of the next chapter. The agreement of purchase and sale included a shareholders' agreement between Victor and the private equity partner, specifying details of Atlas's day-to-day operations, the constitution of the board of directors, and exit provisions—including an opportunity for Victor to consider a buyback. (Appendix C summarizes the deal struck with the private equity group and how it was financed.)

Victor had to make some concessions to the private equity partner, such as giving it the ability to trigger a sale and substantial influence in other major decisions, but he figured it was the price of maintaining a controlling interest. That, after all, was the overriding reason for his decision, because he wanted to see his grandson Stephen running Atlas one day.

DIRECTOR'S SUMMARY *by* Arnie Cader

Once Victor decided to accept the private equity investor's bid, we reviewed the advisory board's composition. Atlas had already gone from a one-man show to a company with an advisory board of four persons. Victor was the chair, Michael Redding was CEO, and Chris Carter was CFO. I sat as an independent director. The board worked well and smoothed Atlas's day-to-day operations during the potentially distracting months of deal-making.

Bringing on the private equity investor, however, would mean another level of formality—a formal board of directors and likely a comprehensive shareholders' agreement. The agreement would set out the board representation for the private equity investor, and would likely also provide that "major decisions" would require the consent of both Victor and the private equity investor; for example, issues such as acquisitions, sales of all or part of the business, financing, dividend policy, bonus incentive programs for executives, transfer of shares among or outside the family, etc. etc.

Part of my job was to make sure Victor understood what the negotiations would entail, prepare him to negotiate effectively, and/or negotiate on his behalf so that the agreements reached would be in his and his family's best interests.

Chapter 5 - Talking Taxes: Making a Good Deal Better

by Steve Landau
Partner
Transaction Tax
Transaction Advisory Services
Ernst & Young LLP

and

Pearl Schusheim
Partner
Transaction Tax
Transaction Advisory Services
Couzin Taylor LLP
(allied with Ernst & Young LLP)

Understanding the Tax Implications

Taxes.

People's eyes glaze over when they hear that word, but we haven't met a business owner yet who didn't sit up and notice that millions of dollars in tax can be saved by structuring his or her affairs one way instead of another. Victor Banks was no exception.

As part of the Ernst & Young Transaction Advisory Services team, Tony Ianni introduced us to Victor to help him understand the tax implications of the various scenarios related to his transition deal (whether he was to sell all or part of his company). This included making sure he understood the tax implications of how his affairs were currently structured, as well as the alternatives for maneuvering within that structure.

Victor had a long and close relationship with his accountant, Paul Stenson. Understandably, he wanted to know how our team—which focuses solely on tax structuring for transactions—could work with Paul on two fronts:

1. To add value to this process by minimizing tax on a deal, and
2. To help optimize the tax aspects of the Banks family's wealth.

Our transaction tax practice group, with various offices across the country, provides tax advice for buyers and sellers of businesses and for companies that want to make their corporate structures more tax-efficient. Steve spends a great deal of his time advising owners of larger private companies who are completing substantial monetization of their wealth. Pearl is a lawyer; she combines corporate and personal tax planning with estate planning in advising business owners.

The Estate Freeze and the Trust

The first thing Victor wanted help with was cleaning up the trust mess. He was referring to the estate freeze he'd done fifteen years earlier and the trust that had been set up at the time. Paul Stenson had reminded him that in six years, the twenty-one-year rule, applicable to trusts, would kick in and there would be a deemed disposition of the assets in the trust that would create a huge tax liability—unless he gave most of the Atlas shares held by the trust to the kids before the 21st anniversary due date.

It seemed as though Victor expected us to have an answer on the spot—an impossible expectation. We told him we'd need to study all the relevant documents to understand how the freeze was done, how the trust was set up, and the intentions at that time. We'd need to look at Victor and Anne's wills to understand how they were structured. And we'd have to talk further with him and Anne to get a fuller picture of their situation and future objectives. We also told him it would make sense to deal with these issues while completing the tax planning for the upcoming transaction.

"I just want you to fix this so I don't pay a fortune in taxes and so my kids don't get almost $200 million dollars worth of Atlas common shares in six years. It could ruin Atlas if one of them wants to cash out. I don't see what our wills have to do with that," said Victor in one of our first meetings.

It was an understandable point of view for someone focused on a very particular problem. Victor was specifically

ON THE SHOULDERS OF ATLAS

worried about the tax rule that deems most trusts to have disposed of their assets at fair market value every twenty-one years. For assets that have a gain, such as the shares of the Atlas holding company in the trust, the deemed disposition would result in a capital gain—and, in the case of the family trust, a big tax bill.

One way to avoid triggering the gain in these circumstances is to distribute the appreciated property—in this case, the holding company shares—to some or all of the trust's beneficiaries before the twenty-first anniversary. Although that would defer the tax bill, it would put shares directly in the Banks children's hands.

"Victor, I know the trust is a big concern and that you'd like to avoid getting hit with an excessive tax liability and your children receiving all that value in Atlas shares," said Steve. "But before we can make any reasonable suggestions, we need to understand what you want to accomplish. We can't look at the trust in isolation. We need to see it as part of the overall structure of your affairs. And we also need to look at the different ways you can structure the sale of Atlas, because the structure you choose will affect how the various parts of your family's wealth are allocated."

Victor turned to Pearl. "Pearl, tell me: Isn't he making this more complicated than it needs to be?"

"Think of it this way, Victor: The result of our work is tax savings, but the work itself is *tax planning*. It can't be done well in one-off bits here and there. Good tax planning is like a thousand-piece, three-dimensional jigsaw puzzle—every piece has to fit exactly in the right place. Think of tax planning as a foundation that supports and holds all the pieces together. So I have to agree with Steve. Let's look at your options and see which structure meets your overall objectives best."

What Are Victor's Tax Options?

While Tony was working to identify potential buyers and investors, we took the information Victor gave us about what he wanted from the sale of Atlas and worked out different scenarios that would each meet his goals. Luckily, we were involved long before the letter-of-intent stage; this gave us an advantage in determining exactly what deal structure would be best for Victor and furthering the negotiations in that direction.

We spoke many times with Victor about the various options and their advantages and disadvantages. We wanted him to understand things from a tax perspective, of course, but we also wanted to make sure he understood the bigger picture—things such as how much cash he'd be able to take out under each scenario, which family members could receive that cash, how much flexibility he'd have in directing future investment income, and how much control he'd retain in his company.

These were the four options for Victor to consider for restructuring Atlas and disposing of all or part of his interest:

1. Old Holdco would sell all of the Atlas shares to Acquireco for a combination of cash and shares of Acquireco. This would be taxed at a higher rate than some of the other options.

2. Atlas would sell all net assets to Acquireco for a combination of cash and Acquireco shares. The assets to be sold would include the shares of the US subsiduary. There might be more tax on this type of sale, but the buyer and the Banks family would get the tax benefit of amortizing the assets and goodwill based on their current value, which might allow for a higher negotiated sale price. There might also be third-party agreements and contracts that could complicate the sale of assets.

3. Victor and the Old Trust would sell the shares of Old Holdco to Acquireco for a combination of cash and shares of Acquireco. Too much cash would end up in the Old Trust and not enough in Victor's pocket.

4. Victor and the Old Trust would transfer the shares of Old Holdco to RealtyCo. Then Realtyco would sell the Old Holdco shares to Acquireco for a combination of cash and Acquireco shares. This option achieves a very favourable tax rate, less than half the normally applicable rate. It could also be structured so that a disproportionate share of the cash would go to Victor and permit a share restructuring to deal with the current accrued value in the Old Trust. It would also address the future growth in the retained interest in the business, ensuring that it accrue or grow in favour of a New Trust that could benefit a broader family group than was included in the Old Trust.

As we showed Victor diagrams illustrating the various potential structures, he interrupted us. "Old Holdco this and New Holdco that, and Old Trust this and New Trust that, and Acquireco this and Rolled Equity that! Do you two ever speak plain English?"

"Sorry, Victor, but it's hard to talk about these things without using those terms," Steve said. "Let's just look at how things stand right now. You control a holding company that owns 100 percent of Atlas common shares. That's Old Holdco. Fifteen years ago, you froze the value of your own interest in Old Holdco, and indirectly Atlas, which was then $40 million.

"You've already talked about the result of that freeze, but let's go over it again in a bit more detail. You now hold preferred shares of Old Holdco valued at $40 million, and that value can't change. The trust created fifteen years ago with your children as beneficiaries—we'll call it the Old Trust—now holds all the growth in value since that time in the form of common shares of Old Holdco, and they're worth the difference between the $40 million that Atlas was worth then and what Atlas (net of debt) is worth today, plus the $6 million of cash and marketable securities that Old Holdco has."

"And no matter what happens, a new company—Acquireco—will likely have to be created to purchase the business or the shares of Atlas or Old Holdco. So when we use the term 'Acquireco,' we're talking about the buyer you'd hold an interest in as well," said Pearl.

We needed Victor to understand that you can work within the constraints of a particular ownership structure in different ways to get the after-tax return you want from the deal.

"Of course, under any structure you choose, we'd make sure you trigger only a taxable gain on the cash you receive and get a tax deferral on the part of the Atlas value you continue to hold in equity of the company," said Pearl.

Victor wanted to hear more about the idea of an asset sale. "Generally speaking, one potential advantage to you in an asset sale is that a buyer may be willing to pay more because it may get a significant future tax benefit," Steve explained. "The buyer can amortize goodwill and can also amortize the assets to the extent that it's paid more than the assets were depreciated down to.

"Another advantage, assuming you retain a 65 percent interest in the company, is that you'll reap a proportionate amount of the benefit of that amortization. A potential disadvantage is that you'll end up paying more tax on the sale than in some other scenarios. But when you look at the higher price the investor may pay because of its future tax savings and your share of the future tax savings from the goodwill amortization, it's still a fairly attractive tax result.

"With this structure, we also need to pay careful attention to the additional commercial complexities that may be associated with an asset sale, which may include getting permission from suppliers and customers to transfer business contracts to Acquireco. These could include supply agreements with customers and suppliers as well as any leases for the Canadian operations that would be carrying on Atlas's Canadian business."

Victor thought that could be messy and wanted to hear about the other options. He looked a bit queasy when Steve explained that one result of the third option (in which he and the Old Trust would sell Old Holdco shares to Acquireco for cash and Acquireco shares) could be that cash wouldn't end up in the right place. "You could end up with too much cash in the Old Trust, for example, and not enough in your own hands."

"That's definitely a nonstarter!" Victor said.

We talked at length over several weeks, answering Victor's questions, explaining the nuances of the various approaches and gradually learning about the man and what he wanted. Even though our work is technical and complex, its purpose is straightforward and uncomplicated: to arrive at the right structure for a deal to meet the client's objectives most fully and most tax-effectively.

Victor was dealing with a lot throughout this period. By the time he was closing in on his final decision—sale of 35 percent of Atlas to a private equity partner, using the structure described in the fourth option—he'd been working with Ron and Ken for several months to figure out the optimal management structure for Atlas and to put the pieces in place that would strengthen his management team. He'd made sure Tony got all the information he needed, then dealt with interested bidders' due diligence requests. Victor and Anne had also been sorting out some thorny family and estate issues with Linda Betts (see Chapter 7) and talking to Sheila Crummey about their wills (see Chapter 9). And the whole time, Victor was still running Atlas.

Just What *Is* Wrong with the Old Trust?

As we reviewed all the freeze and trust documents, and Victor's and Anne's wills, a couple of things became clear, especially that Victor and Anne hadn't done adequate estate planning. The simple wills they'd drawn up, in which each left all assets to the surviving spouse, constituted all they had in terms of an estate plan.

As Victor himself said, he hadn't paid enough attention to the trust's details because he was more focused on growing his company. He'd liked the idea of passing on some of his company's value to his children and reducing the taxes payable on his death. But he hadn't thought about whether he was too young for a full freeze to make sense. After all, he'd been only fifty-four at the time and had always been in excellent health, so the statistical likelihood of his dying before the twenty-first anniversary deemed disposition of the trust was relatively small. He also hadn't done a really rigourous forecast of Atlas's potential value in twenty-one years.

It had been already evident that his son Robert, twenty at the time, was having personal difficulties. But Victor hadn't fast-forwarded in his mind to Robert at forty-one and the fact that the trust could give him, along with Victor's other children, a significant stake in Atlas—in all likelihood, as it now appeared, a more significant stake than Victor himself would be left with. The trust wasn't structured to protect against Robert accessing and dissipating the assets, and it lacked some other protections that would have meant that neither Robert nor any other child could demand that the company buy their shares for cash.

Victor realized that without doing some other planning as part of the deal, there were two broad alternatives for dealing with the assets in the Old Trust: either leave the assets in the trust and pay about $45 million in tax or effectively distribute the assets or growth of the trust among the children in some way, which would defer the tax liability until they either sold the shares or died.

Victor's best choice was to structure the sale according to the fourth option (transferring the Old Holdco shares from Victor and the Old Trust to Realtyco, then having Realtyco sell Old Holdco shares to Acquireco for cash and Acquireco shares). It would let him create a structure to put aside a significant part of the cash received from the deal as a nest egg for his retirement with Anne.

Completing a refreeze whereby the growth shares held by the Old Trust would be replaced by fixed-value preferred shares of Realtyco would allow all future growth in the rest of the family's assets to grow in favour of a New Trust that could benefit a larger family group, potentially including Anne and himself and his grandchildren. Victor liked that this option would achieve an attractive tax rate on the cash portion of the deal. It would likely come in at under 10 percent—considerably less than half the usual rate.

The New Trust would have a fresh twenty-one years to deal with its own deemed disposition of assets, and the expanded list of beneficiaries would provide far greater flexibility for dealing with that event well down the road. It could, for instance, help fund an alternative course for Stephen if Atlas were sold before he could assume an active role in the company. Victor could also deal with the twenty-one-year deemed disposition problem for the Old Trust without giving control of Atlas or Realtyco to the children. He could both control that value and determine how to cede control of it in the future.

This structure would also cap the value of the Old Trust's assets at its current value so that at least the twenty-one-year problem would be limited to a fixed amount and not be a moving target, as Atlas's value was expected to increase over the next six years. The Old Trust's trustees would have to be satisfied that the transaction was beneficial to the Old Trust's beneficiaries. As the value of the shares held by the Old Trust was being fixed, it might be that the shares the Old Trust received should have a fixed dividend right, or some other benefit could be given to the Old Trust.

But what would happen in six years? Wouldn't the kids still get their hands on preferred shares that they could demand be turned into cash? Pearl explained a couple of options for dealing with this concern. For example, the Old Trust could enter into a shareholders' agreement with Victor and Realtyco restricting the circumstances under which the holder could demand redemption of the preferred shares. After the Old Trust distributed the preferred shares to the kids in six years, they would be bound by the terms of the shareholders' agreement that the Old Trust signed. Other options involved more complex arrangements, and these could be considered in due course.

Victor looked relieved and said he understood the importance and value of getting advice from people who deal with these things all the time.

Why was the fourth option the best? You can review the Banks family empire's full structure in Appendix D, but we'll mention some highlights. Using this structure and reorganizing the ownership of personal assets as we recommended would provide a triple-whammy win, giving Victor the greatest amount of after-tax proceeds, dealing effectively with the issues surrounding the Old Trust, and setting up the right structure to minimize tax on the future sale of all or part of the family-retained interest in Atlas.

It would give him about $35 million in personal money to provide financial comfort for Anne and himself, and this money wouldn't have anything to do with what the Old Trust owned or what the New Trust would eventually own. They could take a trip around the world or do whatever else they chose with it, and if the business failed for some reason, they'd still be financially set.

This strategy would retain a significant part of the cash proceeds in Realtyco, which could be invested in a portfolio to provide for the family's future needs and help fund Victor's retirement. In addition, Realtyco would not only have a significant pool of capital ($80 million in cash and marketable securities, including the $6 million previously in the Old Holdco), but also own the real estate related to the business, from which it would get rental income.

The benefit of an estate freeze is to not only reduce the tax that's paid on future appreciation but also pinpoint what the tax liability will be so you can figure out how you'll pay for it—or perhaps even reduce it over time.

Victor would hold super-voting shares of Realtyco, giving him control of the decision-making about use of its assets. So seen as a whole, Realtyco, Old Trust, and New Trust made up a neat little package including all the family's wealth, other than what Victor would take for himself and Anne.

DIRECTOR'S SUMMARY *by* Arnie Cader

Steve and Pearl spoke to Victor about possible ways to structure a transaction with the private equity investor. As an advisory board member and trustee, I used my experience as a lawyer, businessman, trustee, and business consultant to review the alternative structures carefully.

I've found that tax advisors can create efficient but complex structures to pay the least taxes. But in doing so, they sometimes propose structures that distort companies' everyday operations. I'm generally wary of esoteric and off-the-wall strategies, such as forming companies in the Cayman Islands or Ireland. You can imagine some of the aggressive planning that can be proposed. I like a good balance of tax efficiency with what's best for the operations of the business and what's best for the family.

That's why I like working with Steve and Pearl—because they have the same philosophy about how a deal should be structured—and that's why I liked the fourth alternative that they put forward. Victor and I discussed all the alternatives at length, and I encouraged Victor to make the decision he made.

TRUSTEE'S MEMO *by* Arnie Cader

The trust created at the time of the initial freeze had been obviously set up primarily for tax purposes, without much thought as to how it would work for the family down the road—especially if Atlas went on to become a highly successful company, as it did. I'd say Victor and his advisors were shortsighted in naming only the children as beneficiaries of the first trust and giving them all the future growth in Atlas's value. It certainly would have been possible to include Victor and Anne as potential beneficiaries. Victor could receive value while he was alive, and Anne could receive value after his death. This would have also taken care of Victor's concern about his children acquiring a major stake in the company before he thought they were ready for that financial responsibility.

Victor waited much too long to review the trust arrangement, especially given Atlas's exponential growth. When I told him that his advisors should have urged him to look at it, he said his accountant, Paul Stenson, had actually encouraged him to do so several times over the years, but he had kept putting it off because some pressing business issue had always needed his attention.

This isn't an uncommon problem. Trying to focus an entrepreneur like Victor on a potential family or estate problem several years away is like trying to stop a moving train. That's why it's important for such people to have strong and independent advisors whose judgment they respect, advisors who are confident and aren't employees, people who can stand up to business owners and make them listen when they say, "Look, this needs your attention *now*."

Chapter 6 - Let's Make It Legal: Getting the Deal Done

by Frank A. Archibald
Partner
McMillan LLP

When Victor and I first met, I expected an interview situation in which he'd decide whether he wanted me to do the legal work his pending deal required. I had just told him that I'd be happy to go through my experience and approach, and that I'd also provide references.

I was more than a little surprised when he said, "Forget the references. Ron and Tony have both highly recommended you, and that's good enough for me. Look, I'd normally interview several firms before choosing one, but I've been putting this decision off. Not that I don't know how important it is, but I've never been so busy in my life, what with running the company and talking to consultants every time I turn around. Don't get me wrong—they've been great. I don't know how I'd have gotten this far without them, but this whole process has required enormous amounts of time and energy. Anyway, I'm expecting letters of intent from prospective purchasers, and I need your help with that. I'd also like to hear how you see this deal unfolding and getting done. If I'm satisfied with what you have to say, we can move forward."

"That's fine with me," I said. "I've spoken to Tony, Steve, and Pearl to get a sense of where you are. I guess that's one advantage of working with a group of advisors who work well together—we've got the communication process down pat."

Victor agreed that everyone seemed to work well together and share information efficiently. "And it's not just that. They work really well with my people, too. Paul Stenson and Jonathan Hill—my accountant and my lawyer—told me the other day that they felt like part of a high-powered team. Jonathan doesn't do this type of work, but he knows a lot about the company and needs to be involved. And Chris Carter, my CFO, said he hasn't felt so excited about things since his MBA days. Okay, so what do we do with these letters of intent?"

Tony had already told him that the letters of intent would be more detailed than the earlier expressions of intent and would help Victor decide on a prospective purchaser.

"The letter of intent is an important step in the process that sets out the purchaser's proposed terms. We'll go through it carefully with you and consider likely issues of concern in the share purchase agreement that should be raised now. The point of the letter of intent is to make sure the parties are on the same page and set out the basis for continuing negotiations. It'll contain an obligation to negotiate with the purchaser exclusively, but otherwise, it isn't a legally binding document. Once the letter of intent is signed, the purchaser will continue with its due diligence. Tony will be firming up a term sheet with the lender, and Steve and Pearl will be working through a tax plan both for the sale and afterward. We'd work with Tony and Jonathan to respond to issues raised by the purchaser's further due diligence, but our real involvement is when we need to start documenting everything."

"When we get to that point, I hope everything is settled and the documentation is mostly standard stuff. It shouldn't take much to complete the deal, right?" Victor asked.

I told him that ideally, with the thinking already done, our role would be implementation. I also cautioned him that issues always come up. "Victor, this won't be simple. We're working on three separate transactions. First is the purchase transaction, and we need to get the draft of the purchase agreement. The purchaser will do this draft. We'll have a detailed letter of intent, and hopefully the first draft of the purchase agreement will follow the letter of intent. The purchase agreement will also set out the information that needs to be scheduled. Remember, you'll be making a set of representations in the purchase agreement, and if you don't have them exactly right, you'll be leaving yourself open to a lawsuit.

"Second is the financing transaction: Atlas is borrowing a significant amount of money, and there'll be a detailed loan agreement setting the terms of the loan—we'll need to review that agreement carefully and negotiate to secure the most favourable terms we can.

"Third is the reorganization transaction. We have to be careful with the terms of the documents and the ordering of the steps to make sure the plan works and will survive scrutiny by CRA."

Victor looked weary once I reminded him of everything we had to accomplish. But I had to tell him one more thing. "As part of the purchase transaction, if the purchaser is a private equity investor, we'll need to settle a shareholders' agreement that will set out controls on Atlas after the transaction."

Victor said it sounded like a lot still to do. I agreed that much needed to be done, and said he had to look at this in stages. The work that would go into the letter of intent and the term sheet with the lenders would be a big help in simplifying the process later.

"What can I expect in terms of how you'll be working with me?" he asked.

"One thing we do at the start of a transaction like this is set out a project management plan. We'll get all parties—us, the purchaser, the lender—to agree to the schedule and work together. My role is to keep everything moving to a conclusion, make sure you understand everything that's going on and how Atlas will be run after closing the deal, and make sure you don't get sued after the deal is done."

"That all sounds good. But let's go back to that shareholders' agreement—it's a concern I've had with selling to a private equity investor. I'll tell you something right now—I don't want to be too tied down. I know my business better than anyone else, and I don't want to have to report to a bunch of accountants all the time."

Private Equity Partner: Pros and Cons

I reminded Victor that the private equity investor would be putting a lot of money at risk and therefore would be very concerned about control and having a clear right to an exit.

"You, or Michael as CEO, can maintain day-to-day control, but you won't have control over major decisions. The private equity investor will want to consent to any major decisions—decisions such as a plant in Europe, that acquisition in California, issuing shares, or borrowing money. And the private equity investor will want some control over management's performance.

"The investor will be planning to sell at some point in the next five to seven years. It needs to know that it can be the one to decide when and how to sell. We can build some prior notice requirements into the agreement for you, and try for a mechanism that will give you an opportunity to step in to buy the private equity investor's position, but the investor won't agree to something that will decrease its ability to sell at a satisfactory price."

Victor said it sounded like a lot of restrictions to put up with for someone who would have only 35 percent of the company. I told him there were positives as well and that he needed to buy into the idea of having a partner. The private equity investor would contribute to the growth in the value of the 65 percent of Atlas that Victor still owned. I reminded him that this 65 percent represented the bulk of his and his family's wealth, and that he needed to protect and maximize its value.

"The private equity investor has financial and management expertise that can be a catalyst to introduce changes that will move Atlas ahead. One of those changes will be the board's composition.

You'll have to operate with a board of your nominees, plus the people the private equity investor nominates."

"Operating with my current advisory board is easier than I thought it would be."

It was good that Victor felt that way because many entrepreneurs find a board of directors a waste of time. But entrepreneurs who get the right people on the board and are willing to be flexible and learn to work with a board generally find it to be a huge benefit.

Victor said Arnie had already taught them a lot about how to make the board work, and he hoped Arnie would also guide them through working with the private equity representative—or representatives—on the board. I said it sounded like he had some good people, and I encouraged him to think seriously about adding someone of his choosing who had deep industry experience. I also cautioned him that the private equity investor would want to review and approve the independent board members.

Victor looked at his watch and asked if I needed anything else from him.

"We need to identify the contact people at Atlas—we need someone from the company to take the lead on the purchase and financing transactions, principally in giving directions, and we'll also need an administrative person to help assemble the documents."

Victor said that Chris Carter could take the lead on the purchase and financing transactions, and he'd find someone for the administrative tasks.

Tying Up Loose Ends

A couple of months went by, and we were close to getting done. There had been several meetings, some of which went on longer than Victor would have liked, but all issues had been settled and most documents drafted. Victor called me to say he wanted to meet with me and Anne.

Victor wanted to talk about family issues—particularly, how he and his family should handle matters of control for Realtyco in the future. Because of these family issues, he wanted Anne in the meeting. By this time, Victor and Anne had met with Linda Betts and Sheila Crummey several times to deal with family and estate concerns (you'll read about this in upcoming chapters).

There were many things to think about. Luckily, most issues regarding Realtyco didn't have to be decided right then because Victor and the trusts held Realtyco's shares and Victor would control Realtyco through his voting shares for the foreseeable future.

I reminded them, though, that another major event would occur in five to seven years, a significant one for the family: One way or another, the private equity investor would be selling its interest. If the family were to sell at the same time, it'd be left with a pool of money. If, however, the family bought out the private equity investor, or if the private equity investor's interest were sold to a third party or through an IPO, the family could still have a significant investment in Atlas. It would be easy to split up a pool of money if the family wanted, but much harder to split up the investment in Atlas.

"The original idea was for you to step back from day-to-day operations. I think Anne will agree that there's nothing wrong with you maintaining ultimate control through your voting shares of Realtyco, but you should start actively involving others in decisions now. You and your family will have to decide whether to sell out with the private equity investor or stay involved. And you shouldn't make that decision alone. You and your family are deferring the sale decision for now, but you really need to keep people thinking about whether the family should ultimately sell or not. The family council may be a good place for these discussions to take place.

"Second, if the family decides they want to stay involved after the private equity investor sells, you need to realize that, ultimately, control will shift away from you at your death, if not before. So it makes sense to take steps to let others make decisions now, to see how things work out, rather than to wait until you die and potentially leave Anne and the kids in a mess."

"Does that mean a shareholders' agreement at Realtyco like the one at Atlas, where I couldn't do anything significant without the private equity investor's consent?" Victor asked.

"At some point, and certainly before the shares of Realtyco are distributed out of the Old Trust, a shareholders' agreement would be important, but not right now. At the moment, the only shareholders of Realtyco are you, the Old Trust, and the New Trust," I said.

"Once the sale takes place, Atlas will have an independent, working board. You'd do well to consider a board for Realtyco composed of you, Anne, Anthony, and one of the Old Trust's trustees—most likely Arnie. It makes sense for your family council to have input into how Realtyco operates, and Anthony could provide that input on the family's behalf. You'll need a shareholders' agreement in place before distributing the shares to the children, at minimum to restrict the transfer and redemption of the shares and possibly to provide for sale options. This should be discussed with the children well in advance of the shares' distribution."

"Well, maybe," Victor said. "I could let the board of Realtyco make some decisions and see how they work out. It could be a good training ground for them."

I suggested that maybe it was time that his children experienced some of the advantages of ownership, as opposed to simply employment.

"What do you mean by that?" he asked.

"The directors of Realtyco, together with the trustees of the Old Trust, could consider an annual distribution policy. So in addition to earning income from Atlas, the children would get some return on their investment. It could also show how the family council, the trustees, and the board work together. The family council should have some input into how much is distributed. The board of Realtyco would have to agree, and if they agreed, they'd then have to manage Realtyco's resources to produce the income stream for the distributions."

Victor said he'd have to get his head around that, but he could see some positives in the suggestion.

"I think it's a good idea," Anne said, after remaining silent and listening intently for the meeting's duration. "You know, having the children receive some income from the investment might help keep the family together. If there's no money to make them feel like owners, someone might get frustrated and want out."

She paused for a moment, then added, "In one way, we view this sale as a way to get money out of Atlas, but it's turned out to be much more than that. It's turning out to be the first step in finally dealing with both business and family issues head-on."

DIRECTOR'S SUMMARY *by* Arnie Cader

Victor has always exercised absolute control over decision-making at Atlas. Now that the transition is in the works, he needs to give some of that control to the people who will be making decisions day in and day out—not easy for an entrepreneur who has always relied on his own judgment. If he maintains tight control, the next generation will never learn to manage the business. Also, by selling part of Atlas's equity to a private equity investor, Victor now has a partner he'll have to learn to work with and get the best out of.

There's control in law, and then there's control in fact. Let's look at law first. When an issue comes up for discussion at a board of directors meeting, the directors vote on that issue. As chairman, Victor has only one vote there; he could be defeated easily. Owning the multiple voting shares, and with a proper shareholders' agreement, he'll have the right to appoint and remove a certain number of directors. Furthermore, as stated previously, the shareholders' agreement will ensure that both he and the private equity investor, as shareholders, have to approve major decisions. However, he must understand that the directors and the management run the business, not the shareholders. In accepting the board structure and the private equity investor, he gives up absolute control. He could block major decisions, but not day-to-day decisions.

Victor will continue to exert influence simply by the force of his personality and his history with Atlas. If Atlas is to be successful after he's gone, he needs to let others have significant decision-making power and to work with the private equity investor as a valuable partner.

PART III

Solving Victor's Dilemma:
Taking Care of Other Business

Chapter 7 - My Family Is My Business; My Business Is My Family

by Linda Betts
President, The Heritage Wealth Strategy Group Inc.

Defining the Business

The first time I heard of Victor Banks was one uncharacteristically mild February day as I was walking to my office after a meeting nearby. The day had been beautiful, but then a surprise rain shower arrived. I ran for cover, and, of course, my cellphone rang just then. It went to voice mail before I could answer. The message was from Ron Prehogan.

Ron had called me because the family itself seemed directionless amid the massive changes taking place within the family company. Ron had been urging Victor to see how I might help, but Victor kept saying, 'I'm trying to sell a business. I don't need any touchy-feely family therapy stuff.' But Victor did an about-face and wanted me to talk with him and his wife.

Ron filled me in on what he'd learned about the family, and we met with Victor and Anne not too long after I received that message. It was immediately clear that Ron had guessed correctly when he said Anne's influence had probably convinced Victor to hold the meeting.

The first thing Victor said was, "I want to be frank. As I see it, I've got a major company here. I built it, and my main concern recently has been what to do with it. I don't really see why it matters what other people think. In fact, I bet that if you got my family in a room together, you'd get six different ideas of the best way to go. We got a taste of that at the cottage—I assume Ron told you all about that?"

As I nodded, Anne interjected immediately.

"My main concern is our family. In a way, this is no different from how it's always been, is it? You were always involved in the business, and you didn't seem to understand how that affected our family life while the kids were growing up. Now you don't see how your disentanglement from the business may affect our family's future."

"Anne, my family is one thing, and the business is another. End of story."

I had to come in at this point. "Victor, let's look at what's happened. Ron and Ken helped you figure out your business issues and structure, and helped you decide what to do with your business. Steve and Pearl have been working to come up with the optimal structure for your transaction. Tony has identified potential buyers and investors, and you're pretty close to making a decision. As I understand it, you hope your grandson will run the company one day, which remains one main reason for the direction of your decision. So what will it be worth if your family implodes in the meantime—if, in fact, there isn't a solid commitment from your children and they decide they don't want any part of the plan?"

That must have got Victor to see the very real connection between his business and his family, because suddenly the conversation's tone changed.

"Tell us how you operate."

I started with the result my process is designed to achieve. "My concern when I work with a business family is to preserve and nurture *all* family assets. Ron may have told you that I used to practise law. I'm not a practising lawyer now, but I use my legal experience in a consulting role as a family wealth strategist to help families address their wealth in its broadest sense."

This piqued his interest.

"You call it *your* business, Victor, and you have every right to. But my guess is that your children call it the *family* business. If you're like most successful business families, your business defines your family in profound ways: It provides their livelihood, it provides a sense of personal identity, and it provides a sense of common identity. Sure, the business is your largest financial asset, but other assets are just as important in the context of the family.

"Think about an entrepreneurial enterprise like Atlas. It's been successful because it's always been inspired and led by your vision, and it's always been run to that vision. The same is true of the most successful, biggest public companies in the world: They're successful because they're working to a vision.

"The same business principles that apply to the business world apply to families as far as their operation and success are concerned. A family needs to develop and work to a strategic plan. It should understand and apply *all* of its capital, not just one aspect of it, to a vision that everybody understands. I help business families define that vision, create their strategic plan, and ensure that the business asset promotes what's important to the family."

"You know, we've always been comfortable," Victor said. "We've provided a good life for our children. But we've never had this kind of money before. It may sound funny, but we're concerned that the enormous value they'll receive from the trust in six years might not be that great for the kids. We're afraid this sudden wealth could disrupt their families if they don't deal with it responsibly."

This was a good sign because it meant they were genuinely concerned about their family's well-being. It also meant they were at least beginning to grapple with estate-planning issues. The conversation was wide-ranging and gave me valuable initial insights into Victor and Anne, how they saw their family, and what was important to them. They asked many questions of me as well, about how I came to be doing this kind of work, what my process involved, what my fee was, and what success I had in helping families get on track and stay there.

I started to explain my process, and when I paused for a moment, Victor said, "That sounds pretty straightforward. A family meeting to let everyone know what we're doing in the context of our overall wealth and why we're doing it—that makes sense. Individual meetings to get everyone's honest thoughts and feelings. Drafting a report on what you've discovered and giving everyone a chance to vet their own sections—that sounds fair. Then a collective report and a family meeting to discuss it. Is that it?"

"Well, I'd say that covers the background work. The report leads us to your family's strategic plan in connection with your overall wealth. From that, we figure out next steps, including wills, possible new trust arrangements, shareholders' agreements—every appropriate tool at our disposal to ensure the family stays in alignment, both now and as things pass on to the next generation."

They both liked the thought of focusing their family in a more deliberate way and thought my approach made sense. Victor even said that maybe he'd been a bit hasty when he'd called this "family therapy."

As the meeting ended, Victor and Anne said they wanted to set a date for the first family meeting on these issues. Then they asked about Michael, and I suggested we should keep these meetings to direct family at first—recognizing, of course, that the private discussions the children would have with their spouses would inevitably influence their contributions to the process.

I also pointed out that it would have been better to have a strategic plan in place *before* the reorganization process had begun. That way, decisions could have been taken with a clear focus on a predetermined outcome, and everyone's good ideas could have been addressed. There were many unanswered questions about how the Banks family would navigate the near future, let alone become the business dynasty Victor envisioned.

Discovery Meetings

It was in a meeting with Ron that Victor's children first learned about the original estate freeze Victor had done and about the old trust, of which they were the beneficiaries. I had given much thought to how to bring this up, and I had discussed it in depth with Victor and Anne. It's a complicated discussion—how do you talk to children as beneficiaries of a trust valued at almost $200 million without immediately engendering feelings of entitlement and endangering their work ethic?

We decided to explain in carefully chosen words exactly what the words "in trust for" mean. We'd emphasize that the trust was discretionary and that it meant no beneficiary actually would own any of the trust's assets until they were distributed.

Once Anthony, Rose, and Caitlin were comfortable with me and trusted that I was there for the good of their family and not just as Victor's agent, they opened up. In many ways, they were a great family, a strong family. They worked together day in and day out, and they still talked to one another! I've seen many families in which the siblings are barely civil to one another.

New information and insights emerged. Anthony was actually the kin-keeper of his generation. His difficulty with Michael was based not so much on jealousy of Michael's talents and unabashed ambition (though there was certainly an element of that) but more on anger and frustration at how Michael took Rose for granted. This sort of thing happens often—bad feelings between family members get played out in the business even though they didn't originate there. Anthony also knew more about Robert's problems than anyone else, though he'd kept what he'd known to himself.

Caitlin made a personal, revealing, and ultimately important statement. "What I might want to do is what my mother did—raise my children and be part of my family. Now that I'm pregnant, maybe I'll have a chance to do that. But if you're not in the business, as far as Dad is concerned, you're not part of the family. Just look at Robert—my father doesn't have the time of day for him."

Why was this important? Because it brought to light the fact that, in this family, there was no recognized, articulated, safe way to say, "Hey, I don't want to work in the company."

Anne's concerns about Rose's marriage were well-founded. Rose told me she thought the marriage was salvageable, but she wasn't 100 percent sure.

Robert remained a wild card. He was affable and charming but didn't give much away except that he "requires" a lot of money to live and wasn't earning income consistently because "the right job hasn't come along yet." Robert was clearly a special case.

Anne confirmed much of what Ron had told me about her and confirmed my first impressions of her. She was deeply committed to her husband and family, and she sometimes felt these commitments pulling her in two directions. I also learned how important her volunteer work with the Canadian Mental Health Association was. She said, "I guess most people have a reason for the charitable causes they choose, don't they? Robert is my reason."

Victor and Anne said that they wanted all the children to be treated equally, but they were concerned Robert might squander any wealth that came his way.

"I'm also worried Robert could be disruptive as a major shareholder. I don't want the people working in the business to be distracted, and I think Robert could make a real nuisance of himself if he becomes a major shareholder," said Victor.

Anne especially wanted Robert to have a chance to engage and invest in his own future. They decided that if he didn't—or couldn't—advance, he might have an equal financial opportunity, but the form of his entitlement would be different than that of the other children: outside the business and/or in a life trust. This was more of a tendency toward fairness than toward absolute equality.

Deciding to Move Ahead Together

Anthony's attitude became much more open as the weeks went by. He's actually the one who summed things up well at the second family meeting when he said, "Look, it's too bad Robert's circumstances changed so that he couldn't join us for this meeting. I know we're all concerned about his well-being, and I know, you, Linda, will keep him updated and engaged in this process. This process has been tough at times, and sure, we've hashed over things we didn't like in the past. But that's the past.

"This is about who we are now and who we want to be in the future. And one thing that's clear to me is that we want to move ahead together. We want some individual financial autonomy and liquidity, and we need a plan to achieve that. It's one way to help ensure our collective harmony when it comes to our wealth.

"Most of us have a good work ethic, and we want to make sure that having liquid wealth doesn't undermine it. We have to develop tools to sensibly manage, keep, and grow our wealth. And we all believe it makes sense to give back intelligently to our community, which means developing a plan to do it strategically. I feel confident we're on the right track."

Victor said he felt confident, too. But what exactly did moving ahead together mean? To what issues and decisions was Anthony referring?

Finances were the first thing. Victor and Anne's need for financial independence had gotten the ball rolling in the first place, and it was clear that the private equity deal would take care of that. The family wanted to keep the bulk of their financial assets together, at least for the foreseeable future. To do that, they understood the benefit of the Old Trust and the importance of putting certain agreements in place and doing proper planning to keep things running smoothly.

They'd already worked out compensation agreements with Ron and Ken for people in key management positions at Atlas. In my discussions with the family, Caitlin had asked, "But what happens to me if I decide I don't want to go back to work after my baby is born?"

Those discussions were excellent because they gave Caitlin a safe environment to think about what *she* really wanted to do.

In discussing her role at the company, she saw that other family members felt she was important there, and they said they were eager to help her balance her life as a mother and an active contributor to the business. In the end, she chose—without any pressure—to continue in her role at Atlas.

Then there was discussion about the fact that some children might want to be more involved in the business than others. This meant we needed ways to keep business and family separate, yet let passive shareholders have a voice. Ultimately, we'd need a shareholders' agreement that would allow for a sanctioned exit from the business by specifying the rights and responsibilities of both passive shareholders and management shareholders. It would address how a passive shareholder could be "taken out" or trigger his or her own exit.

Marriage agreements are a touchy subject even before people get married, let alone when they've been married for years! Though it was Rose's marriage that was shaky, she wasn't singled out in the discussion about marriage agreements. The premise was that any marriage can break down and that measures should be in place to preserve family assets among direct family members. We'd need to get these marriage agreements in place before any assets were distributed from the Old Trust.

This led to an important discussion of trusts and wills.

"You've made a lot of progress toward defining yourselves as a family," I said. "One thing you need to do is give careful thought to who should be the trustees of the Old Trust, the New Trust being set up as part of the reorganization for the private equity deal, and any possible new trusts that might be set up, including trusts established in wills.

"You need *real* trustees who are committed to the family and will deeply engage with family members to help them learn the tools they need to manage this wealth and make good decisions. The right trustees might also be mentors and even sit on the family council. And you need to update your wills. There are many things to think about when it comes to your wills—and yours especially, Victor, needs to address what happens with your voting control of Atlas."

The family was still in transition on the importance of ownership versus control. Victor had promised Anne that he'd step back from day-to-day operations within two years. Part of Victor's comfort in transitioning control will come from his role as chair of the board of directors. Hopefully, more comfort will come from his confidence that, with independent people sitting on the board, one or more independent trustees, and a properly set-up family council, his family will be able to make sound decisions and act on them.

Regrouping regularly and re-evaluating the plan to keep it true and on task is part of my ongoing role and is essential to success.

DIRECTOR'S SUMMARY *by* Arnie Cader

Victor asked me what I thought about creating a shareholders' agreement for Realtyco and asked about the advisability of marriage agreements.

At the moment, Realtyco's shareholders are Victor, the Old Trust, and the New Trust. I told him having a shareholders' agreement when the Old Trust distributed shares to the children would be essential. I recommended waiting a few years to let the family get used to the new business structure. Then discussions could be opened up among Victor, the Old Trust's trustees, the New Trust's trustees, and the children. Though the children aren't currently shareholders, it'll be important to obtain their input well before the distribution of the shares. When he asked what should be included in the agreement, I said the two most important considerations for the beneficiaries of the trusts were

1. Whether they would get any income distributions from Realtyco, and

2. What would happen if they decided they no longer wanted to be involved in the business—i.e., was there any liquidity to their beneficial interest in Realtyco through the trusts?

Therefore, the shareholders' agreement needed to deal with these issues of income and ownership. Regarding income, the shareholders' agreement needed to address a Realtyco dividend policy so people would know what to expect to receive each year from their trusts, or, in Victor's case, from his shares. Regarding ownership, the family would have to decide how to compensate a family member who chose to leave the business. The shareholders' agreement also needed to deal with the management responsibilities of those involved with the business, and with their compensation.

Victor thanked me and said, "That's pretty much what Linda suggested, as well."

Ideally, each beneficiary should enter into a marriage contract to protect the value of the shares received from the Old Trust from a claim in the event of marital breakdown. Though it's difficult to negotiate a marriage contract *after* marriage occurs, it may be possible to do so if the terms are limited to protecting the shares from a claim for equalization and if support rights aren't addressed. Making the marriage contract a requirement for a distribution of shares from the Old Trust may motivate the spouses to come to a reasonable agreement.

TRUSTEE'S MEMO *by* Arnie Cader

Linda touches on the important role of directors and trustees as potential mentors. With independent people on the Atlas board of directors, independent trustees, and a properly set-up family council, individual family members can turn to several people for advice.

Clearly, one reason to have independent and experienced board members and trustees is so they can educate the individual beneficiaries on business in general and on the family business in particular. Often, beneficiaries have never worked with lawyers or accountants before, and, as a trustee, I'm in a good position to help them understand how and when lawyers, accountants, and other professionals should be involved, what their role or roles are, and how to select professionals with whom they would be comfortable. I can also offer advice on appropriate remuneration for the services they'd be providing.

Independent directors and trustees can also teach family members about the differences between a 100-percent family-owned company and a company that has non-family shareholders. It's a different situation, and directors and trustees with the requisite experience can be invaluable to the family members as they make such an enormous transition.

Chapter 8 - I Invested My Life in My Business—How Do I Invest the Proceeds?

by Susan Latremoille
First Vice President and Wealth Advisor
The Latremoille Group, Richardson GMP

Defining the Goals

I was slightly early for my first meeting with Victor and Anne. Victor's assistant led me to his office. She said he was in another meeting and might be delayed, but Anne would arrive momentarily.

The first thing I noticed about the office was the Group of Seven paintings on the wall. I was so enthralled with them that I didn't hear Anne come in. When I turned, she was already extending her hand.

"I'm Anne Banks," she said, "and you must be Susan."

Just then, Victor also arrived, so after introductions, the three of us sat down at the worktable occupying a corner of the office. Anne turned to me and said, "Susan, we've been talking to several people about how to manage the money that will come from the sale of part of Victor's company. I've pretty much taken care of things on the home front for years while Victor has focused on Atlas. Not just raising the kids and running the house, but money matters, too. I'm the one who mostly deals with our bank manager and the financial advisor who manages our investments and our RRSPs. Perhaps you can start by telling us what you think we should do with this windfall."

77

"Well, I really don't know what you should do with it," I said.

Anne tilted her head to one side and looked at me with as much attention as I'd given the paintings moments ago.

"That is, I don't know *yet*. I look at money as an enabler—not as an end in itself, but as a means to an end. So what you do with your money isn't really the start of the conversation. The start of the conversation is what you want your money to do for you."

I put a copy of my first book, *The RichLife: Managing Wealth and Purpose*, on the table. I told them the title indicated a lot about my approach. "As I see it," I said, "managing money is extremely important work. Managing money so that it supports the purpose of people's lives is even more important. And that's exactly what I try to do for my clients."

Here we had a good discussion about the relationship between a client and a financial advisor. We agreed about the basic elements of that relationship:

- *It should be a relationship of mutual trust and respect;*
- *It should be based on the advisor's thorough understanding of the client's circumstances and objectives (conversations with and reports from Ron and Linda had been helpful in this regard); and*
- *Ideally, it should be long-term.*

I asked their permission to start our conversation about their wealth with a question I ask all my clients: "If you can imagine yourself on your deathbed, looking back on today, what would have to have happened for you to feel you've lived your lives without regrets?"

Deciding What Matters

Victor hadn't really said anything up to this point, but as you might imagine, this question got us into a lively discussion.

"I've finally come to the point where I'm looking forward to retirement and travelling with Anne. She's already got our itinerary planned for five years after I retire!" Victor said. He was also eager to become more involved in the Board of Trade and wanted to own the little peninsula across the bay from their cottage so that no one could build on it.

Perhaps his most important wish was to rebuild relationships with his kids. "I've been the proverbial busy dad. When I check out, nothing would satisfy me more than knowing my kids feel about me the same way I felt about my father. It may be too late, but it's not too late to try."

At the end of her life, Anne wanted to be able to look back on the intervening years as an idyllic time spent with Victor. With a little laugh and a glance toward Victor, she added, "Time when his first priority is finally me, not Atlas."

She said she would love to establish a personal art collection. Eventually, it could even become a philanthropic gift when she died. She made it perfectly clear that she'd also continue her volunteer fundraising work for the Canadian Mental Health Association.

Both Anne and Victor said they wanted to maintain their lifestyle, and they wanted to look back on healthy and happy children and grandchildren, and maybe even great-grandchildren. It didn't matter much what they chose to do—doctor, lawyer, teacher, politician, sculptor, musician—so long as they led full, productive lives.

"One thing that's really important to me," said Victor, "and I know it's important to Anne as well, is that we not squander this money. We're finally at the point that we've been working toward, each in our own way, since we got married. I'm handing off Atlas now, and I'm hoping it'll work out, but I realize I can't count on the company to support us. And with these equity guys in the picture, things are different now—no dividends while they're involved, salary and bonus restrictions, stuff like that.

"The best thing for our peace of mind is to look at this money as our payoff and assume it's all we'll have. We want to live well, but we also want to find a way to preserve this capital for our children and grandchildren."

"And for some charitable causes," Anne said. "I couldn't agree more with Victor that we should plan as if Atlas won't provide more for us. Maybe there will be more, but better not to be presumptuous and plan on it."

What they were telling me is what I hear from most clients, though everyone expresses the idea in different words: They want to live well now and in retirement, to give back to their families and communities, and to leave a legacy.

"You know, it's funny. It's such a different feeling—having real, hard cash and not just a valuable company," said Anne. "I feel richer and less secure at the same time. The thought of so much money, and the responsibility of managing it, requires a different mindset, doesn't it?"

Victor agreed that the sale made him feel different, too, and partly for the same reasons. He said it also made him feel different in a peculiar way because he saw it as a turning point in his life. He'd always been a builder, and now he wasn't sure what he was going to be.

"There's one more thing you need to be aware of," Victor said. "I could have sold the whole company. There were interested bidders, and they seemed willing to pay a good price. But I decided to go with the private equity option because I want to keep the possibility open that Atlas will stay in the family. I'd love to see the day my grandson takes over."

Though he might be planning to retire from day-to-day involvement in Atlas, the company still occupied a big space in his mental life.

"Victor, I certainly understand your desire to keep it in the family, and I also understand the issue of planning the intergenerational flow of your nonbusiness assets," I said. "After all, I work for a private company started by the fifth generation of the family. Richardson GMP has a successful history of shepherding family wealth from one generation to the next. Wealth management is our only business."

Where Do We Go from Here?

We talked at some length, and they filled in more details about their desires and their concerns. We got more detailed about their exact income needs, and again they stated their wish to preserve capital. As the meeting ended, I outlined the next steps for them.

I'd follow up with a letter recapping their goals, the strengths of their situation, and the opportunities it afforded them, and any potential barriers to meeting their goals. This would be an opportunity to ensure that I'd heard them accurately and noted everything they thought was important. The letter would also outline action steps to move the process to the next stage.

"I'll also translate the information you've given me about what you want your money to do for you into an investment policy statement," I said.

An investment policy statement (IPS) is a document laying out a plan for attaining financial objectives. It considers preferences and constraints expressed by a client and includes a recommended asset allocation, a breakdown of how money should be invested in various asset classes. In addition, the client receives an investment plan outlining my recommendation for his or her portfolio.

I stressed that there's no cookie-cutter element to how we manage our clients' money. Each client is different, and each has an individual portfolio designed specifically for his or her circumstances. My firm has no proprietary products, so I have no vested interest in what is recommended. I also assured them that I consider constant communication with my clients essential to the relationship. Circumstances and objectives may change, and the portfolio may need to change to reflect new realities.

"How can you possibly keep on top of so much for every client?" asked Anne.

"When you work with me, you are able to pass on the responsibility of coordinating your investments' details," I said. "My team is a highly trained and dedicated group of people. We understand what's involved in keeping on top of clients' affairs, and we're proactive about it.

"As an example, we stay in touch with clients' accountants to remain aware of their tax situation so we can make effective, tax-based portfolio changes where appropriate. We run projections for clients to answer questions such as, 'How would it affect my ability to meet long-term objectives if I were to withdraw X number of dollars to help my daughter buy a house?' We *know* our clients and keep the lines of communication open so clients know everything they want and need to know about their investments."

Anne seemed relieved to know I had a lot of professional support built into how I manage my clients' wealth. If, after reading my follow-up letter and reviewing their IPS and investment plan, Victor and Anne agreed that the approach made sense and wanted to engage my services, we'd move on to implementing the recommendations.

Their situation, as they described it, put enormous pressure on their assets. I asked permission to share the information with a colleague who could bring a complementary strategy to protect their capital while their portfolio generated adequate income. They agreed readily, and I said I'd bring Peter Creaghan to our next meeting.

Victor and Anne also asked about fees. I told them my fees are based on the assets and services we provide and that fees are detailed in subsequent meetings.

As I was getting ready to leave, Anne said, "Susan, I'm sorry, but I wonder whether it might not be better to have several financial advisors—you know, give one-third of the money to three advisors instead of all of it to one—spread the risk a bit."

This idea of spreading risk among multiple advisors is one that many people share, but it generally works against them.

"Anne, let me tell you how I manage risk. First, we decide on the appropriate asset mix, and then I engage different, carefully chosen money managers to manage different portions of your portfolio. Let's take the growth part of the portfolio as an example— the equities in the portfolio would most likely include Canadian, US, and international equities, both large and small companies, and exposure to emerging markets. A small but still significant part of your equity portfolio would be invested in alternative asset classes such as hedge funds for protection against undue currency or market fluctuations, and real estate limited partnerships and private equity funds for additional diversification. Each part of the portfolio would be managed by different people, and I'd be monitoring on an ongoing basis to ensure the overall portfolio remains true to your objectives.

"Now imagine what happens if you have three advisors. First of all, there isn't likely to be any communication among them. The result? Duplication. You may end up with too much money invested in the same stocks, or too much invested in certain markets, or not enough invested in certain geographic regions. In other words, you can actually *increase* your risk by forgoing careful coordination of your investments."

Anne thanked me for the thorough response. "That's certainly one way of looking at it. I hadn't considered these issues."

Combine and Conquer

Julius Caesar's famous "divide and conquer" strategy may have worked in the Gallic Wars when he sided with individual barbarian tribes in disputes with local rivals, but my quarter-century of investment experience has taught me that combining strengths with other professionals makes much more sense when faced with complex financial challenges. This collaborative approach is essential when dealing with the needs of the very wealthy because their particular circumstances require the knowledge and experience of highly specialized experts. Combining strengths is exactly what Peter Creaghan and I did, and we met with Victor and Anne the following week.

Victor and Anne's needs had two elements:

1. The need to generate substantial cash flow from their investments and
2. The desire to preserve their capital.

We presented an integrated strategy to address both issues, combining a specialized investment portfolio (my area of expertise) with the innovative use of insurance vehicles (Peter's area of expertise, which will be described in more detail in Chapter 10).

"Insurance!" Victor cried out at one point. "I've just sold one-third of my company for over $100 million in cash. Insurance is the last thing I need more of!"

Many people have misconceptions about insurance, and Victor's is an objection we're used to dealing with, but it was Anne who redeemed the moment. "Let Susan and Peter explain further. I told you I did my homework. Her firm deals exclusively with the issues of very wealthy Canadian families, so I'm not surprised to hear things from them we didn't hear from others."

We knew what financial return we needed to accomplish, so Peter and I had jointly prepared and presented several different scenarios for them to review. We showed them the following:

- *The numbers if they pursued things either one way or another,*
- *Where the money would come from for their ongoing living expenses, and*
- *Where the money would come from for the requisite insurance policy that would preserve their capital.*

We also explained how much insurance they'd need to satisfy their estate goals and how that affected the asset allocation for the management of their money. We took everything into account—all their existing assets, including their RRSPs, individual and joint accounts, Victor's cash from the private equity sale and his interest in Realtyco, the trust—and showed them how everything could work together to accomplish their goals.

The option Victor and Anne liked best required about a 60/40 split, investing half of their assets in fixed income securities and half in equities. The fixed income portion included a significant investment in insurance, as well as fixed income investment vehicles. The equity portion could be distributed across different investments under the direction of several money managers, as I'd explained to Anne earlier.

Like many people in their situation (business owners who have never had a lot of liquid assets), Victor and Anne were leery of putting so much money into the public securities markets. I assured them once again that I follow the principles of diversification in all my investment planning, and the recommended portfolio reflected this. It looked much like the one I described to Anne at the end of our first meeting. (See Appendix D for a detailed summary of their portfolio.) I suggested, though, that the actual investments could be made monthly over a period of a year to avoid investing all at once, at what could turn out to be a peak in the markets.

Victor and Anne decided our approach made sense. We arranged a follow-up meeting for the next week.

Chapter 9 - What Should My Estate Plan Look Like?

by Sheila M. Crummey
Partner
McMillan LLP

When I met with Victor and Anne Banks, I already had good, solid information about them and their family from conversations with Ron Prehogan, Linda Betts, and Arnie Cader as well as documents they'd given to me. I had a good sense of their family members and how the family functioned, and I understood how the family viewed the business.

Having this knowledge beforehand was a tremendous advantage. Because I was already aware of their wishes to some degree, I was aware of some of the hot spots and could give initial thought to some of the will-planning issues—all before we sat down to talk. This is more information than I often have when meeting a client for the first time, but even with this background, verifying the information through a direct conversation was critical. So Victor and Anne and I had a lengthy, detailed discussion one morning in Victor's office. I started by asking them about their family, about their children and how they got along with one another, and about their children's spouses and grandchildren.

Victor said immediately, "You should ask Anne about all that. She's the one who always gets things firsthand. Anything I know, she knew first." I assured Victor I was as interested in his views and feelings and, slowly but surely, he started contributing his perspective on things.

Taking Care of Rose

When they talked about Rose, they mentioned how concerned they were about her marriage's viability. Linda had recommended they strongly encourage not only Rose but also Anthony and Caitlin to enter into marriage agreements with their spouses to protect assets in case of a marital breakdown. They'd consulted with Arnie about this and also asked Ron and Frank for their opinions. All agreed that marriage agreements should be signed before distribution of assets from the Old Trust.

"We definitely want to protect what we leave to Rose in our wills. We don't want half of it to go to Michael if their marriage does eventually break down," said Anne. Victor quickly seconded the sentiment.

I assured them that inheritances are generally protected under Ontario family law. However, the protection would be lost if the inherited assets were invested in a home or a cottage or inherited assets were put in joint names with the other spouse. Rose's ownership of substantial assets would increase the risk of Michael making a claim for support.

"There's a way to build protection into your wills to minimize these risks, but you'll want to discuss it with Rose and make sure she's comfortable with it before deciding," I said.

I was glad to hear them say they planned discussions with all their children before inking their wills. When planning an estate, it's best to have everyone aware of the intentions informing the will's creation.

Victor wanted to know why I'd suggested talking to Rose specifically about this. I told him this was because it would mean that her inheritance wouldn't actually be hers outright.

"No, no, no. Hold on there," he said. "What do you mean, it won't be hers outright? You're saying we leave it to her, but it's not hers? I don't get it. I didn't work like I have to *not* leave something to my kids!"

Anne said she didn't really understand that line of reasoning, either.

"One technique we could look at is using a discretionary lifetime testamentary trust," I explained. "We'd name Rose as a beneficiary of that trust, and her children and potentially her grandchildren. That's what I mean when I say her inheritance wouldn't be hers outright. She and the other beneficiaries would have the *benefit* of the assets but not *ownership* of them. We'd protect the assets from Michael by simply not naming him as a beneficiary. That way, if their marriage breaks down after you've both died, Michael wouldn't have access to the assets."

"Yeah, but couldn't he sue and make a case that he's entitled to half of her assets?" asked Victor.

I explained what would happen in that case. "Let's say Michael did take a run at the assets. He says Rose has X millions of dollars that she inherited and those dollars should be split between them. The testamentary trust creates significant roadblocks, and such lawsuits are rarely successful. Why? Because, legally, the assets aren't Rose's; they're assets of a trust of which she's one of several beneficiaries, so she has no legal claim to them. It's up to the trustees to decide whether to make any payments to a beneficiary and if so, how much and when to pay.

"I've explained that income distributed to Rose from the trust may affect her support obligations to Michael, but the trustees can manage that risk by choosing not to distribute income to her. For example, if Rose decided she wanted a vacation home, the trust could purchase it for her use rather than give her the cash to buy it herself."

Victor liked that idea, and asked if this type of trust had other benefits.

I told him how it's more tax-effective than leaving the assets directly to Rose. "The trust would be generating income, and Rose and her children would be entitled to that income. The income earned in the trust can be split among Rose and her children, so the money that goes to the children gets taxed at their progressive tax rates, which presumably will be less than Rose's tax rate. The amount they save this way may seem small in the overall scheme of their wealth, but it's another tool that can be used to shepherd the money."

"That all sounds pretty good," said Victor. "Is there anything else?"

"Another advantage of a discretionary lifetime testamentary trust is that it provides protection from creditors. From your vantage point today, you can't know what creditor issues your children or grandchildren may have in the future. Under this structure, no creditor can say they have a claim to Rose's money because she owes X number of dollars. Rose would have only a discretionary entitlement to the assets, which may or may not come to fruition. So, like Michael, that creditor would have nothing concrete to go after."

The final benefit of this structure, I explained, is that it would also defer the decision about how the assets are to be distributed among the grandchildren.

What to Do about Robert

By the time the conversation came around to Robert, I felt like an old family friend. That's not my role, of course—I have to be objective to best serve the client's interests. But when people share deep family secrets, it's hard not to feel some connection. So I was taken aback when Victor said, "We'll have to see what Rose thinks about this discretionary lifetime testamentary trust, and maybe even Anthony and Caitlin, too. But it sounds perfect for Robert, whether he likes it or not."

I was about to remind them what I had said earlier, that I strongly recommend people talk to their heirs before deciding these things, when Victor turned to Anne and said, "Listen, Anne, we need to be honest with Sheila about him. Can you tell her what's happened?"

Anne's eyes started to well up. She hesitated, dabbed at her eyes with a handkerchief, composed herself with a deep breath, and said, "Oh, goodness. I knew we'd have to talk about this. I just didn't realize how hard it would be. We haven't even had a chance to tell Linda yet. We got a call last night from Robert. He's been arrested for possession of cocaine."

"Possession with intent to sell," Victor added.

Anne continued. "Yes, intent to sell. There was a lot of it in his possession when the police stopped him. He told me how much, but I don't remember. Sheila, you have no idea how heartbreaking this is. I've been helping Robert out financially for some time, and to think he was taking my money and . . . what do they say? . . . putting it up his nose? Putting it up his nose! He assured me on the phone that he's not a drug pusher, though. He said it was just for his personal use."

"As if that's supposed to reassure us or something!" Victor interrupted. "'Yeah, Mom and Dad, I have all this cocaine and it's all for me!' I know people. I'm pretty sure I can get the charge dropped to simple possession, but only on condition he goes to rehab."

"That's what Victor means, Sheila, when he says 'whether Robert likes it or not,'" said Anne.

I told them I was sorry to hear their news, and asked what they hoped to accomplish by setting up such a trust for Robert.

Victor said he didn't want to see Robert squander a substantial inheritance. He didn't want to give Robert the means to destroy his life. He wanted to know whether, if they established such a trust with Robert as a beneficiary, they also could make Robert's ex-wife and son beneficiaries. I explained that they could name any beneficiary they wanted.

"Isn't it odd to exclude one child's spouse from a trust and to include another child's former spouse?" asked Anne.

"Anne, I've been helping people with their estate planning for many years. One thing I've learned is that there's no 'odd' when it comes to wills. Each family is different, and the wills they create reflect that. Many parents believe their wills should provide for each child in exactly the same way. They usually want to be fair to their children, and that's commendable. In their minds, 'fair' means 'equal.' But my experience shows me that 'equal' is sometimes actually unfair.

"You can be flexible and set things up differently for each child, or one way for two of them and another way for the other two. That's why I encourage an open discussion between parents and children without the spouses present. It's best to have families on side with the overall plan."

Robert's arrest, difficult as it was for Victor and Anne, awakened them to the realities of their son's life. They weren't sure they could rely on Robert to fulfill his responsibilities to his ex-wife and son, and they wanted to ensure they'd be provided for adequately.

We talked a bit about the Old Trust and the value the children would get from it. Victor said there was no way he would let Robert get his hands on those valuable Atlas shares—at least, not unless he recovered from his drug problem. Anne understood Victor's point of view—even agreed with it—but was concerned about being fair to Robert. I suggested considering giving less to Robert from the Old Trust (which Robert would have to get outright) and giving him more through a trust, or trusts, that would be established under their wills, which would ensure fairness and protect what he'd receive.

Planning for Victor and Anne

At one point, Anne turned to Victor and smiled. "I can see the gears turning. Are you thinking this might be the way to leave things to me, too?"

"If I die before you do—and let's face it, we'd have to beat the statistical odds for things to work out differently—I don't want you to be left without enough money to support you for the rest of your life."

"Yes, but you know I don't need a fortune."

This led to a good discussion about what should happen when Victor died. For many couples, this discussion is difficult, not only because the impetus for it is the thought of the spouse's death, but also because they often disagree about what should happen. It was obvious, though, that Victor and Anne weren't far out of step with one another.

He'd at least given some thought to Anne's needs after his death. She saw the general shape of what she wanted to happen as the family wealth passed from her to her children, but many details needed working out about how that wealth should pass to Anne in the first place.

Victor pretty much agreed with her when she said, "I'm not planning to live high off the hog, you know. We don't live that way now; why would I suddenly change my lifestyle? Besides, I'd like to make sure our wealth gets passed on to the children and grandchildren. And I don't think I'm being a Pollyanna when I say it's important that some of our money do something for the greater good."

I reminded them of the substantial wealth their children would receive from the Old Trust—wealth above and beyond what they'd be leaving to them through their wills.

They discussed many different what-if scenarios. Anne was genuinely surprised when Victor suggested that she might fall in love with and marry someone else after his death. She immediately dismissed the suggestion.

"Victor has a good point, Anne—that often does happen," I said. "When you're doing will planning, you want to include the family's needs, and as time goes by, the family can include new people. So Victor's point is valid. The question now is, how do you want to structure things knowing it's a possibility?"

"A very remote possibility," Anne insisted.

What did they decide? They didn't make any final decision in that meeting, but I did leave them with several different structures to consider. The idea they thought would meet all of Anne's needs included leaving some assets directly to her to ensure an acceptable level of financial independence, and leaving some assets to her in a spousal trust and in a family trust.

A family trust could be created in Victor's will with the investment assets, and the beneficiaries could include Anne, Robert, Robert's ex-wife, and Robert's son. Victor's will would make it clear to the trustees that he intended Anne to receive primary consideration in their decisions about the assets. Robert and his family would receive payments from this trust before Anne's death if she didn't need the payments for her support.

At Anne's death, all of her assets, all assets remaining in the spouse trust (except the voting shares of Realtyco), and all assets remaining in the family trust under Victor's will would continue to be held in a trust for Robert and his family. This would equalize Robert with his siblings, who would receive approximately equivalent value from the Old Trust and the New Trust, which hold shares in Realtyco.

Anthony, Rose, and Caitlin wouldn't inherit any value under Victor's and Anne's wills. Their inheritance would come from the Old Trust and New Trust, which hold shares in Realtyco and indirectly in Atlas.

The assets left to Anne, either directly or in trust exclusively for her, wouldn't be taxable until she died. Both the spouse trust and the family trust would be good vehicles to split income because each is a separate taxpayer with its own set of marginal tax rates.

"And," Anne said, "it would also protect the assets in case I became disabled or my judgment started to slip as I got older, wouldn't it?"

Anne would be exclusively entitled to all income in the spouse trust and could receive income and capital from both the spouse trust and the family trust. Victor liked that her needs would be primary and that Robert and his family could also be taken care of. They could receive payments from the family trust while Anne was alive and from all of the remaining assets in Victor and Anne's estates at their deaths; these assets would continue to be held in trust for Robert and his family when Victor and Anne were gone.

The spouse trust would also hold Victor's voting control shares of Realtyco. Since one of the spouse trust's major assets would be the preferred shares of Realtyco, it would be important that control of Realtyco remain with the spouse trust's trustees while Anne lived. At Anne's death, these shares could be distributed to Anthony, Rose, and Caitlin, or they could be redeemed, effectively passing control of Realtyco to Anthony, Rose, and Caitlin, who would receive the majority of value in Realtyco when the shares held by the Old Trust were distributed to them.

When I raised the issue of who would act as trustees of the various trusts, they said they already had people in mind because they'd discussed the role of trustee in detail with Linda. Often, this is the most difficult decision, one requiring lots of education about what a trustee does, but Linda had laid the groundwork and that made our discussion productive.

Victor and Anne decided that Anne, Arnie Cader, and Victor's accountant, Paul Stenson, who would be trustees of both the Old Trust and the New Trust when the private equity transaction and the reorganization occurred, would also act as trustees of the trusts set up under Victor's will.

As our meeting ended, it was obvious that they needed more time to think and talk things through with their family. We'd started our discussion assuming their combined estates would go to their four children equally. With that in mind, they'd initially focused on Rose's unstable marriage and protecting her inheritance if the marriage broke down afterward. Once they revealed the details of Robert's situation, it became clear that the estate plan needed to change radically.

While they made no firm decision, it was likely that Rose, Anthony, and Caitlin wouldn't inherit under the wills at all. Rather, they'd be provided for under the Old Trust and New Trust, leaving a roughly equivalent amount for Robert and his family under the wills.

TRUSTEE'S MEMO *by* Arnie Cader

One thing often overlooked when people set up discretionary trusts is that they need absolute faith in the trustees' experience, discretion, and judgment. That's why choosing trustees carefully is so important.

Years ago, many trusts were set up with a trust company as trustee, an option chosen less often today. The prevailing trend now is to name individuals as trustees rather than corporate trustees. Victor asked me to be a trustee because he believed I'd bring an objective and independent voice and serve his family's interests well, given my years of experience as a trustee. He believed I'd prove even more useful as my knowledge of the Banks family and the business of Atlas grew.

Most people understand that when they establish a trust, they're entrusting the care of their assets to the trustees. What better reason could there be to make sure the right people are making decisions?

Chapter 10 - Ensuring the Outcome: Innovative Insurance Solutions

by Peter Creaghan
Partner
Creaghan McConnell Group

I first met Victor and Anne with Susan Latremoille, when we combined our areas of expertise to show how an insurance strategy could enhance their overall investment strategy. At that time, the focus was on the $31 million in cash that Victor would receive personally as part of the private equity transaction. They wanted to ensure it would generate adequate income for them in retirement and that its value would be preserved for their children.

Much had changed when I saw them again, and their thoughts had turned toward how their sudden wealth would affect the lives of their children and grandchildren.

I must have caught Victor in a particularly contemplative mood when I met with them a couple of weeks after the investment meeting with Susan. You could tell he'd been mulling over some difficult family issues. He was more talkative than when I'd first met him—I'd say he was even expansive.

The conversations about Atlas's future and structuring his estate seemed to have gotten him focused on family matters, maybe even a bit nostalgic about his own past and how things had changed. We talked a lot about the differences between growing up with little money (and lots of happy times), as Victor had, and growing up with lots of money, as his children had and his grand-children were doing.

He talked about his boyhood and his father's forge and how they'd built it into a small foundry. It was clear that he had enjoyed his childhood and had great affection for his dad.

He shook his head at one point and said, "I remember sav-ing the money my father paid me for working part-time in the forge after school so I could buy my first bike—secondhand—from our neighbours down the street. I loved that bike, fixed it up all by myself, painted it bright red. You would've thought it was new, except we all knew we could never have afforded a brand-new bike back then. Imagine that! All our kids got brand-new bikes practically before they could walk, and their kids—well, they want for nothing. I'm not sure our kids have learned the lessons Anne and I did by growing up with less. I know we're both concerned about what will happen when they eventually get control over all this wealth we've created, especially now that so much more of it is in cash."

Anne chuckled. "Victor, I'm sure Peter has better things to do than listen to you ramble on and on. Besides, if he can actually solve some of our family financial issues as readily as he handled the preservation of our investment money, I'd much rather listen to *him* talk!"

I assured Anne that I enjoyed Victor's reminiscences. For us, these kinds of conversations are an informal but important way of understanding our clients' deepest principles and values. These values are most often at the heart of our recommendations, and I would have enjoyed spending more time listening to Victor's stories, but Anne was clearly signalling that we should begin the business part of the meeting. I'm guessing she'd seen Victor in this sort of mood before and was afraid he'd just go on and on and nothing would get done!

Getting Down to Business

The family financial issues Anne was referring to came from decisions they'd arrived at regarding the Old Trust—namely, to distribute the shares of Realtyco to three of their four children. They realized that Robert, with an active cocaine addiction, wasn't in a position to receive any shares of Realtyco. He was uninsurable, at the very least, and probably in no position to carry out a shareholder's responsibilities. They decided that since Robert wouldn't receive shares of Realtyco from the Old Trust, he'd be equalized through Victor's and Anne's wills. A trust would be created under the wills that would hold the tax-paid assets. This was their way of making sure Robert was dealt with fairly, despite his drug problem. It would also ensure that he wouldn't squander an inheritance or neglect his son's needs, and that he'd be in no position to affect the business. It also meant that all shares of Realtyco in the Old Trust would go to Anthony, Rose, and Caitlin, which would effectively give them the business. Victor and Anne now understood, however, that along with ownership of the shares comes a significant tax liability.

Victor started right in. "Let me tell you, I always believed I'd be successful with Atlas, but I never imagined I'd be so successful that I'd be sitting down with someone to talk about how to deal with multimillion-dollar tax liabilities for my children. It's almost enough to make me want to forget it all and just go back to running my company."

Anne cleared her throat. "Victor, that's not even funny."

"Well, what do you have in mind, Peter?" asked Victor.

"I'm here to talk about some possible insurance solutions for your family, solutions that will ensure their success and the viability of your business long into the future. The way your family ownership plan now works, Realtyco will eventually be owned by Anthony, Rose, and Caitlin. They'll each have a tax liability in their estates of over $15 million at today's values. What happens if one of them dies? Where will the money come from to pay those taxes? What if you're not around to make those decisions? What if—"

"Are you telling me we should buy $45 million of insurance for our kids?" Victor interrupted. "After all we've already done for them, we have to spring for insurance? We're not doing it. They already have enough from Anne and me. They have $191 million worth of shares—and more, as Atlas continues to grow in value. They're not getting any more, and that's the end of it."

"I completely understand where you're coming from, Victor. You and Anne have given your children more than enough to last several lifetimes. However, you've also given them a tax liability to deal with, and we just need direction from you on which option *you* think is the best way to deal with it."

Victor settled down once he realized there would be several options. "But what *are* the options, and how much does $45 million of insurance cost? It must cost a bundle! Where will we get that money from? We've already made a plan for Anne and me for our money, and we don't have any extra. And we can't make the business pay for it—those private equity guys would never agree to that. What exactly are you suggesting?"

Anne chuckled, and interrupted gently enough to let Victor sit back a little and take a breath. "I think Peter's ready to discuss something with us, if you'd just give him a minute!"

"I'm sorry," said Victor, "it's just when the topic of insurance comes up, I get stressed out. It always costs so much money . . . and when do you ever see anything for the premiums you pay? I'd rather buy lottery tickets!"

"I know how you feel," I said, "because most of our clients feel that way before they see how insurance—life insurance, in particular—can work for them. Remember the work we did with Susan? Remember how the portfolio with insurance delivered *more* income for you and Anne than the portfolio without insurance? If we use insurance as an investment, as part of your family's portfolio of investments and financial vehicles, we can increase your value, not decrease it."

I brought out the lifetime income scenario we'd discussed in our meeting with Susan Latremoille to remind Victor and Anne how the product could help them. It showed how their portfolio could generate 15 percent more income for their lifetimes by using a special insurance strategy in addition to their other investments.

After we'd reviewed this, I said, "Victor, the good news is that the way we're now looking at your estate, with what Steve Landau has achieved with the tax and estate structuring, and with Sheila's input about your wills, and knowing your investment strategy with Susan and so forth, there's no real need for any more insurance on your life than what we've already discussed. Your estate is very liquid; your taxes will mostly be eliminated beforehand. There just isn't the need for large amounts of additional insurance.

"Congratulations on that, because many of your business-owning peers who haven't completed the planning you've done will be facing very large insurance acquisitions at a time when they'll be hard-pressed to obtain insurance at all, and when, due to age, the costs will be highest. You and Anne, however, have successfully transferred this problem to your children, where the costs will be much, much lower."

Victor seemed pleased with this, and rightfully so. The planning that had been coordinated with the advisors had likely saved his estate tens of millions in taxes. And who knows what might have happened to the business or the family without that planning?

"Here's what I suggest," I continued. "And I know Susan has talked to you a bit about this already when you discussed investment of the Realtyco cash. When the private equity deal gets done, Realtyco will have about $75 million in cash. You can use a small part of that, say about one-fifth or $15 million, to acquire an investment-type policy for the kids—and it can be owned by Realtyco so the money doesn't have to leave the system. And, as we've seen with the plans we developed for your portfolio, we'll actually increase—not decrease—the value of your Realtyco investments by using insurance. It's not a cost, it's a benefit!"

Victor and Anne both liked the sound of that, but Victor wanted me to show how that would work. I showed them how a

$15 million investment in permanent insurance could actually double the value of their fixed income assets over a thirty-year period *and* provide them with $20 million of insurance on each of the three business-owning children. (See table in Appendix E.) Not only that, but the insurance can actually reduce the tax liability on death.

Anne said she'd been concerned about how the three families would deal with these issues without a plan, and Victor liked the idea of investing some of Realtyco's cash for that protection, especially when I showed him how that investment would likely perform if it weren't insured.

"So, it's like I'm giving them the business, only it's even better, because I'm using part of the business to protect their interests in the future," he said.

We talked at some length about the logistics. Victor laughed when he realized Anthony, Rose, and Caitlin would each have to get medicals, too.

"But even before that, you have make sure the children are on board with this plan," I said.

"Don't worry about that. This will all be part of our next family meeting," Anne said. "Linda and Ron have more than convinced us of how important it is to talk things through—even difficult issues—especially issues that affect Atlas and our family. And let's face it, there's really almost nothing that affects one that doesn't affect the other in some way. The surprising thing is how good you can get at figuring things out once you get everyone talking."

TRUSTEE'S MEMO *by* Arnie Cader

Peter's chapter ends with Anne and Victor convinced of the benefits of talking things through as a family. As a trusted advisor, a trustee has an important role in family communication in two ways:

1. As a confidant for any family member who wants to speak candidly and off the record about any issue affecting the family and/or the business.

2. As an initiator of discussion when the trustee becomes aware of issues that the family isn't dealing with and would rather ignore in the hope that they'll go away.

In my experience, issues that don't get talked about usually don't go away. Rather, they grow and become increasingly divisive and difficult to deal with. It's not always easy to broach these topics with the family, but then, a trustee doesn't get paid for doing only what's easy. A trustee gets paid for doing what's in the beneficiaries' best interests, and, at times, the role can be difficult.

Epilogue

Labour Day weekend, twenty-six months after the Canada Day weekend at the cottage.

Victor and Anne are sitting on the dock in their Muskoka chairs, sipping gin-and-tonics in the late-afternoon sun.

The family has gathered again, but they've all left to get back to the city before the real traffic crunch begins. Anne looks at Victor and says, "It feels good, doesn't it?"

"Yes, I've always loved sitting here in the warmth of the sun."

"Victor, you know that's not what I mean!"

Victor laughs and says, "I know. I was just kidding. It took us a long time to figure things out, didn't it? More than two years have gone by since that Canada Day weekend, but look where we are now: sitting pretty on a pile of dough, the company running like clockwork, and me sitting here, with all the time in the world.

"Those private equity guys didn't waste any time. They've got the company running like a Swiss watch. I always thought I knew everything about how to run a company, but just imagine what I could have accomplished if I'd had their discipline and procedures."

He paused for a moment to sip his drink.

"I thought I'd hate board meetings. I always thought it would be a fight between what I wanted and what they wanted. I've also learned a lot from Arnie about how to make the board work. These guys act like real partners—they want Atlas to succeed as much as I do. Yeah, it was a good decision. I'm glad Tony found these guys."

Anne shook her head in mock disbelief.

"Victor Banks, you'll just never change, will you? It's good to feel financially secure—not just that we have a lot of money, but that it's being managed well under Susan's care. But I'm not talking about money and Atlas. I'm talking about how good it feels that you aren't tied to Atlas every minute of every day, and how good it feels to have our family together without all the tension and turmoil. I'm talking about how much Michael seems to have changed, and how much more at ease Anthony seems—they actually went fishing together this weekend!

"And Rose says things are better between Michael and her—maybe not perfect, but better. I'm talking about how happy Caitlin is to be a mother, with our newest, and maybe last, grandchild. And, of course, I'm talking about Robert and the progress he seems to be making with his life."

There was a little pause in the conversation. All they could hear was the water lapping on the rocks nearby.

"You know, we couldn't have gotten where we are without such competent advisors," Victor said. "We've diversified our family's wealth, we've improved our relationships, we have new senior management at the table, and you and I have our own bit of money on the side.

"I've said it before, and I'll say it again: I don't know how anyone does all that without the counsel we got—right from the start with Ron and Ken getting us all focused on what's best for the company . . . Tony identifying interested buyers . . . Steve and Pearl coming up with a deal structure that covered all the bases and minimized taxes . . . Frank putting all the legal documents together . . . Peter doing things with insurance I never would have thought of . . . and Susan collaborating on the investment strategy.

"And then there's Sheila helping us figure out what we wanted for the family after we're gone, and then showing us how to arrange things. Arnie made sense of the board and gave good advice as a trustee. And Linda basically transformed how our family gets along."

Anne looked at Victor, pleased that they'd come out on top after years of struggling with major decisions that couldn't be taken lightly.

"You're right, Anne," Victor said. "It does feel good. And who knows, maybe things will work out with Robert. It would be great to have him as a fully functioning family member. That would be the icing on our cake."

APPENDIX A:
People in Victor Banks's Story

NAME	ROLE
Victor Banks	Owner of Atlas Plastics. Age 69.
Anne Banks	Victor's wife. Age 67.
Anthony Banks	Victor's oldest son. Age 42. Anthony is a VP at Atlas, in charge of facilities management.
Stephen Banks	Victor's grandson (Anthony's son). Age 20. Victor thinks Stephen has what it takes to run the company some day.
Rose (Banks) Redding	Victor's daughter. Age 40. Rose is the office manager at head office.
Caitlin Banks	Victor's daughter. Age 39. Caitlin is the VP of human resources.
Robert Banks	Victor's son. Age 35. Robert has personal problems and a troubled history. He doesn't work at Atlas.
Michael Redding	Victor's son-in-law, married to Rose. Age 44. Michael is a vice president at Atlas; he has run research and development; now runs sales and marketing.
Paul Stenson	Victor's accountant, a friend of Victor's since university.
Chris Carter	CFO at Atlas. Victor hired him right out of university, and he's been at the company for 20 years.
Jonathan Hill	Victor's lawyer.

THE ADVISORS	THEIR FIRMS
Ken Andrews	Equitas Consultants Inc.
Frank Archibald	McMillan LLP
Linda Betts	The Heritage Wealth Strategy Group Inc.
Arnie Cader	The Delphi Corporation
Peter Creaghan	Creaghan McConnell Group LTD
Sheila Crummey	McMillan LLP
Tony Ianni	Ernst & Young LLP
Steve Landau	Ernst & Young LLP
Susan Latremoille	Richardson GMP Limited
Ron Prehogan	Equitas Consultants Inc.
Pearl Schusheim	Couzin Taylor LLP (allied with Ernst &Young LLP)

APPENDIX B:
Financial Data: Atlas and Personal Assets

ITEM	VALUE
Atlas Plastics enterprise value (based on private equity transaction)	$250 million
Retained earnings	$40 million
Debt	$25 million
Annual sales of business	$200 million
EBITDA	$42 million
Personal cash and marketable securities	$2.5 million
RRSPs	$2 million
Family home in Toronto	$3.5 million
Cottage on Lake Simcoe	$4.0 million
Ski chalet in Whistler, BC	$4.0 million
Holding company	$6 million of cash and marketable securities
Realtyco	Rental property—$18 million, net of mortgage

Note: An estate freeze was done through a family holding company fifteen years ago, when the company was worth $40 million. Victor owns preferred shares valued at $40 million, and a discretionary family trust holds the common shares now worth $191 million. The four children are the trust's beneficiaries. Victor and Anne are the trustees.

APPENDIX C:
The Banks Family Empire before and after the Private Equity Deal

Victor Banks Existing Family Structure

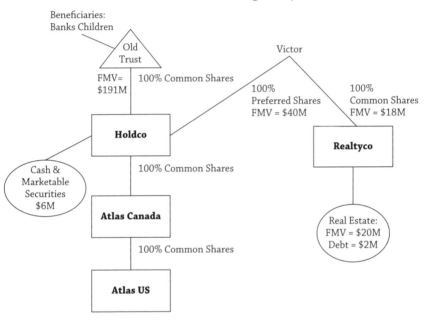

Victor Banks Family Structure
Post-Private Equity Investment

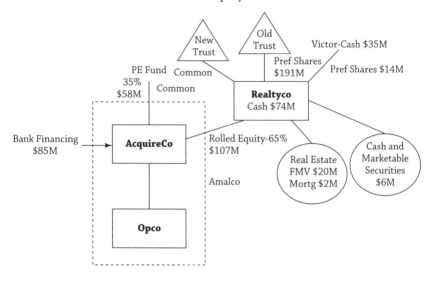

Victor Banks Family Structure
Following Private Equity Investment and after Amalgamation

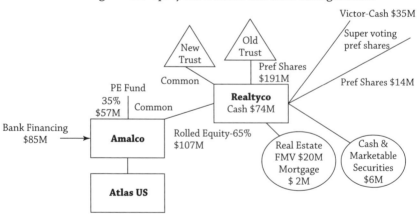

FUNDS FLOW FOR THE ATLAS PRIVATE EQUITY DEAL

Atlas Plastics enterprise value	$250M
Less: Existing debt	($ 25M)
Equity value of Atlas shares	$225M
Atlas Plastics enterprise value-based PE transaction	$250M
Less: New debt to be assumed by Acquireco	($ 85M)
Acquireco equity value	$165M
Allocation of Acquireco to equity value	
• Banks family @ 65%	$107M
• Private equity @ 35%	$ 58M
	$165M
Flow of funds	
• Funds from PI investor	$ 58M
• Funds from new debt provided	$ 85M
	$143M
Less: Funds to pay off old debt	($ 25M)
Gross proceeds to Banks family	$118M
Less: Estimated tax payable	($ 9M)
Estimated after-tax proceeds	$109M

APPENDIX D:
Asset Allocation of the Investment Portfolio

Investment Portfolio for Victor Banks

Recommended Portfolio

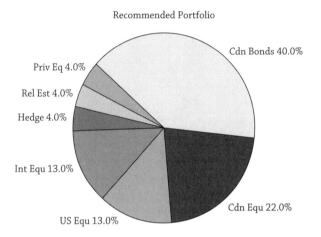

APPENDIX E:
The Insurance Solution

Asset Transfer to Exempt Insurance

Accumulated Capital

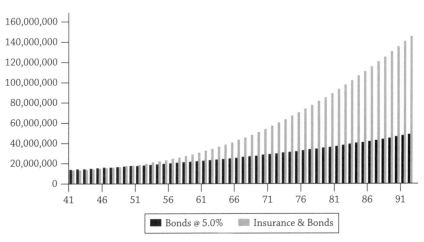

Estate Value

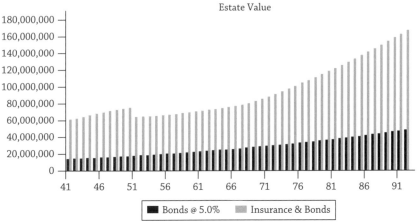

About the Authors

Susan Latremoille, MBA, ICD.D
First Vice President & Wealth Advisor
The Latremoille Group, Richardson GMP Ltd.
www.thelatremoillegroup.com

Susan Latremoille is an award-winning wealth management and investment professional with more than twenty-five years of industry experience. A first vice president and wealth advisor at Richardson GMP Limited, Susan regards managing money as extremely important work—and managing money so that it supports the purpose of people's lives as even more important. The Latremoille Group, founded in 1990, provides an unprecedented level of financial management, investment advice, and personalized service to clients. Susan is also author of the books *The RichLife: Managing Wealth and Purpose* and *It's Not Just About The Money*.

Peter Creaghan, HONS B.A., CLU
Partner, Creaghan McConnell Group
www.cmgexit.com

Peter Creaghan is a partner with Creaghan McConnell Group Ltd., a boutique insurance firm that helps business families to finance their transition plans. CMG provides a unique approach—first by getting crystal clear about the owners' goals, and then by providing solutions to reach these goals at the lowest possible cost. Working in collaboration with their clients' key advisors, Peter and his partners create integrated, tax-advantaged financial strategies. When these are implemented, business families have confidence that their capital needs have been provided for and that they can refocus on what they do best—working on the continued growth of their businesses.

Frank Archibald, B.A. LL.B
Partner, McMillan LLP
www.mcmillan.ca

Frank Archibald is a partner at McMillan LLP and chair of the firm's Toronto business law group. Frank has been an advisor to family-owned businesses throughout his legal career. His practice focuses on providing business law advice to private companies—particularly advice on acquisitions and financings, joint ventures, family business succession planning, and specialized shareholder and business structures. Frank has also handled a number of shareholder disputes involving family members. Frank's experience in dealing with a variety of situations as a transactions lawyer enables him to anticipate thorny issues and provide practical, realistic advice and solutions.

Linda Betts, BA, LL.B, TEP
The Heritage Wealth Strategy Group
www.hwsg.ca

Linda Betts is a family wealth strategist and coach. As founder of The Heritage Wealth Strategy Group, she works with families to identify their strengths and characteristics (their "true wealth"), capture and adopt family philosophies and plans, provide an integrated approach to true wealth management and succession planning, and address complex human issues involved in the intergenerational transfer of true wealth. A former partner at McCarthy Tétrault (and head of its Trusts and Estates Group from 1991 to 1999), Linda is experienced in personal tax and trust planning for high-net-worth families and in cross-border and international tax planning. With more than thirty years of experience, Linda is a frequent speaker, teacher, and trusted adviser to several families.

Arnie Cader, B Comm, LL.B
President, The Delphi Corporation
www.delphicorp.ca

Arnie Cader practiced corporate and business law at Goodmans LLP for twelve years, following which he moved into the business world as executive vice president of Four Seasons Hotels for seven years. For the past twenty years, he has acted as a corporate director and chairman of several public and private corporations, charitable foundations, and not-for-profit organizations, and as a trustee and executor for some of Canada's leading business families. Using his experience as a lawyer, businessman, trustee, and consultant, Arnie has served in senior management and executive roles, assisting his clients in operating their businesses and in their family planning. In this capacity, he has been responsible for negotiating a wide variety of complex business and personal issues on their behalf.

Sheila M. Crummey, LL.B, TEP
Partner, McMillan LLP
www.mcmillan.ca

Sheila Crummey is a partner at McMillan LLP and has been certified as a specialist in estate and trust law by the Law Society of Upper Canada. Since her call to the bar in 1984, Sheila has focused her practice exclusively on personal tax, estate planning, and family business succession planning, and she is a trusted advisor to many families with significant business interests. Sheila's expertise in structuring tax-effective philanthropy has been integral in assisting many clients in creating and managing private family foundations, as well as in establishing endowment funds at public foundations.

Anthony (Tony) Ianni, CA
President, Ernst & Young Orenda Corporate Finance Inc.
www.ey.com/ca

Tony Ianni brings over twenty years of experience in corporate finance services to public and private entities. As president of Ernst & Young Orenda, Tony leads a group of over sixty-five dedicated full-time professionals focused on providing transaction advisory services relating to mergers and acquisitions, divestitures, alliances, and financings to clients contemplating transactions and helps them identify potential buyers and investors. As a former successful entrepreneur himself, Tony knows that building healthy, transparent relationships with his clients and their other advisors is key to maximizing value for his clients.

Stephan (Steve) Landau, CA
Partner, Transaction Tax, Ernst & Young LLP
www.ey.com/ca

Steve Landau is a partner in the Transaction Tax group in Ernst & Young LLP's Toronto office and has extensive experience with the tax aspects of mergers, acquisitions, divestitures, and restructurings. Having practiced exclusively in the tax field for twenty-five years and in transaction tax for ten years, Steve devotes his time solely to providing creative tax-planning solutions for corporate acquisitions, divestitures and reorganizations. A primary focus of his practice is developing and implementing tax strategies for completing the sale of entrepreneurial businesses in a tax-effective manner and blending those concepts with a family's wealth and estate-planning objectives.

Ron Prehogan, B.C.L, LL.B
President, Equitas Consultants Inc.
Partner, BrazeauSeller LLP
www.equitasconsultants.com

Ron Prehogan is a lawyer and the president of Equitas Consultants Inc., which he founded to address a gap in services provided by traditional Canadian estate planning professionals. Focusing on transitions rather than transactions, Ron and his team guide business owners through a customized and proprietary succession planning process that addresses both business and family issues. Equitas' advisory and facilitation services in the areas of ownership and leadership transition, family communications, and dispute management are designed to help multigenerational companies maintain and grow shareholder value while preserving family relationships.

Pearl E. Schusheim, LL.B, LLM
Partner, Couzin Taylor LLP (Allied with Ernst & Young LLP)
www.ey.com/ca

Pearl Schusheim is a partner of Couzin Taylor LLP (allied with Ernst & Young LLP) in the Transaction Tax practice in the Toronto office. Pearl has practised for twenty-eight years and has considerable experience working with business owners, high-net-worth clients, and their families. She has structured and implemented a diverse range of tax plans, including acquisitions, divestitures, financings, and reorganizations, in both domestic and cross-border contexts. In advising private clients, Pearl helps them develop innovative and effective plans that balance their business, tax, estate planning, philanthropic, and personal objectives, devising structures that may involve corporations, trusts, and partnerships.

INDEX

A

acquisition of businesses by
 strategic buyers, 31,
 33–34
advice, *see* process consultants
advisory boards, 24–26, 38–39,
 75–76
 see also trustees
appreciated property
 distributions, 43
assessment process of
 succession planning,
 17–19
asset allocation of investment
 portfolio, 117
asset sales, 44, 46

B

beneficiaries
 discretionary lifetime
 testamentary trusts,
 88–90, 94–96
 discussion of trust terms
 with, 69–70
 insurance planning for,
 99–102
 trust structures and, 20–21,
 45, 48–49

bidding, debt structure of
 business and, 34
board of directors
 control and, 60–61
 formal creation of,
 37, 39
 independent members of,
 24–26, 38–39, 75–76
 post-sale nominations to
 board, 56–57
 terms of sale and, 38
bonuses, 37
budgets, formal, 37
business acumen, 9–10
business performance forecasts,
 31–33
business planning and personal
 issues, 23–24, 69
business skills recognition, 10
business transition experts,
 see process consultants
buy-back options, 38
buyers' restructuring options,
 44–47

C

CA (confidentiality agreement),
 33, 35
capital, *see* wealth
capital gains, 42–43
cash
 debt leveraging of equity
 and, 34

cash—*Cont.*
  investment strategies,
    84–85, 101–102
  liquidity of business assets
    and, 7
  restructuring options for
    sale of company and,
    44–47
  selecting a strategic buyer
    and, 37
charitable giving, 79, 80
chemistry meetings, 15–17
children, communication with
  parents and, 11–12, 19,
  69–70
CIM (confidential information
  memorandum), 33–35
co-CEOs as red flag, 36
collaborative approach to
  financial management,
  83–85
common problems, effective
  framing of, 22–24
communication
  among children and parents,
    11–12, 19, 69–70
  need for honesty and, 18,
    102–103
  between spouses, 7–8
  trustees and, 103
company health and
  interpersonal problems,
  23–25
compensation, determination
  of, 24, 37

competitors as strategic buyers,
  31–32
concessions in sale of
  business, 38
confidential information
  memorandum (CIM),
  33–35
confidentiality agreement (CA),
  33, 35
consultants, *see* process
  consultants
control and leadership
  transitions, 60–61
controlling interests and terms
  of sale, 29–30, 37–38
corporate financial planning
  preliminary options
  meeting, 27–30
corporate structure transitions,
  25–26
customers, 31–32, 46

D

day-to-day operations, 38
debt structure of businesses, 34
decision-making
  leadership transitions and,
    22–25, 58–61
  private equity investors and,
    56–57
deemed dispositions, 7, 42–43
discretionary trusts, 88–90,
  94–96

distribution policies, 59–60,
72–76
diversification, portfolio
management and,
82–83, 85
dividend payments, 37
dreams of the future, 18–19
due diligence
exclusive negotiation periods
and, 37–38
gathering information for
sale of business and, 29
of interested buyers, 36

E

earnings forecasts, 37
employment agreements and
sale of business, 31
EOI (expression of interest), 35
equity, debt leveraging of, 34
estate freeze
benefits of, 50
tax implications of, 7, 20–21,
42–43
trust structure and, 45–50
estate planning
insurance for beneficiaries
and, 99–102
marriage agreements and,
88–90
for surviving spouse,
92–95
trust structures and, 47–50

working with estate
planners, 87–88
exit provisions, 38
expression of interest (EOI), 35

F

facilitators, *see* process
consultants
fairness and equality of
estate planning, 91–92,
94, 99
family business advisors, *see*
process consultants
family businesses
effect of business on family,
65–68
family councils and, 24,
58–59, 72–73
leadership transition
assumptions, 9–10
learning from parents and,
3–4
role of family members in,
10–11, 69–70, 71–72,
80–81
strategic wealth planning
and, 66–67, 71–73
family dynamics
assessment of present status
and, 18
as defined by family
business, 67
favoritism and, 11

family dynamics—*Cont.*
  implications of sale of
    business on, 58–60
fee arrangements with process
    consultants, 29, 82
feelings, 18, 69
financial performance forecasts,
    31–33, 48
financial planning
  corporate financial planning,
    27–30
  potential scenarios for, 84–85
  for retirement, 6–7, 20–21,
    121
  strategic family wealth
    planning and, 66–67,
    71–73
  summary of Atlas Plastics
    financial data, 111
  see also investment
financing transactions, 55
forecasts of business
    performance, 31–33, 48
formal business sale processes,
    37–38
freeze, *see* estate freeze

G

get-to-know-you meetings, 15–17
global expansion of business, 6
goodwill amortization, 44, 46
growth of business, 4–6

H

holding companies, 43–47

I

independent board directors,
    24–26, 38–39, 75–76
information-gathering process,
    16, 22–26
inheritances, 7, 88–90,
    99–102
insurance
  as investment, 100–102, 119
  misconceptions about, 84
  preservation of wealth and,
    84–85
  reflections on life and,
    97–98
  tax liability of beneficiaries
    and, 99–102
interpersonal problems and
    company health, 23–25
investment
  insurance as investment,
    100–102, 119
  personal priorities and goals
    for, 77–81
  portfolio management,
    82–83, 85, 100–102, 117
  realty companies and estate
    structures, 50
  risk and, 82–83

working with a financial
advisor, 81–83
IPS (investment policy
statement), 81–82

J

job descriptions, 37

L

leadership development
programs, 24
leadership transition, interviews
of family and key
management, 21–22
lease agreements, asset sales
and, 46
legacies, *see* estate planning
legal advice, specialized, 36–37,
41–42
letter of intent (LOI), 36,
37, 54
liability recognition, 23
lifestyle and succession
planning, 17–20
liquidity of assets, 71, 74–75, 85
listening, 6–7, 12, 97–98
loans and financing
transactions, 55
LOI (letter of intent), 36,
37, 54

M

major decisions and
shareholders'
agreements, 39
management of company, 24
management personnel,
24, 31, 56, 71
marketing documents for sale of
business, 33–35
marriage agreements
estate planning and,
88–90
strategic family wealth
planning and, 72
trust structures and,
74–75
meetings
for family wealth strategic
planning, 69–70
with interested buyers,
35–36
for transition planning, 16,
22–26
minority positions and partial
sale of business, 29–30

N

navigators, *see* process
consultants
negotiation, exclusive periods,
37–38

O

objective advice, 25–26
outright sale of business,
    28–30
ownership of company, 24,
    71–73

P

parents, family leadership
    transitions and, 9–12,
    19, 21–22
partial sale of business, 28–30
partnerships, 5
personal issues and business
    planning, 23–24, 69
philanthropy, 79, 80
portfolio management, 82–83,
    85, 100–102, 117
preliminary options meeting
    for corporate financial
    planning, 27–30
priorities, 11, 79
privacy and information-
    gathering interviews,
    16, 21
private equity investors
    concerns of, 33, 34
    flow of funds from purchase
        of business, 115
    partial sale of business,
        28–30

pre- and post-sale financial
    structure, 113–114
pros and cons of selling
    business to, 37–38, 56–57
as source of capital for
    business, 7
process consultants
    collaboration among, 83–85,
        105–107
    estate planners, 87–88, 87–88
    family wealth strategic
        planning, 65–76
    fee arrangements with,
        29, 82
    financial advisors, 81–83
    independent board directors
        and, 25–26
    sale transaction lawyers,
        36–37
    selection of, 7, 12, 15, 25, 28,
        53–54
    transition planning overview,
        15–26
project management process for
    sale transactions, 55
purchase agreements and
    transactions, 55

R

realty companies as part of
    estate structure, 45,
    48–50

recognition of personal
    liabilities, 23
reorganization transaction
    documentation, 55
respect, 15, 16
restructuring options overview,
    44–47
retirement planning
    financial planning and, 6–7,
        20–21, 121
    personal priorities and goals
        for, 77–81
risk
    financial management and,
        82–83
    perceptions of business
        volatility and, 32–33

S

safeguards, trust structures and,
    48–50
sale transactions
    financing of, 55
    purchase agreements, 55
    reorganizations, 55
    review of proposed
        structures, 51
    specialized legal advice for,
        36–37
    tax implications of different
        sale structure scenarios,
        43–47

selling a family business
    evaluation of what-if
        scenarios, 17–19
    involvement of owners with
        process, 32–33
    management team
        involvement with
        process, 31
    negotiation period, 37–38
    pre- and post-sale financial
        structure, 113–114
    preliminary options review
        meeting, 28–30
    selecting a buyer, 37–38
    spousal involvement with
        process, 30
sense of identity, family
    businesses and, 65–68
shareholders' agreements
    leadership transitions and,
        58–61
    redemption of shares, 49
    structure of trusts and,
        73–76
    terms of sale and, 38, 39,
        55, 56
spouses, communication
    between, 7–8
strategic buyers (strategics), 31,
    33–34
strategic planning
    discovery meetings for
        family wealth planning,
        69–70

strategic planning—*Cont.*
    family commitment to,
      70–73
    management personnel
      and, 24
    sense of identity and family
      businesses, 65–68
    shareholders' agreements
      and, 73–76
success fees for sale of
    business, 29
succession planning process
    overview, 15–17
suppliers as strategic buyers,
    31–32
suppliers, asset sales and, 46

T

tax issues
    complex nature of, 42–43
    deferment of tax liability, 43,
      46, 48
    discretionary lifetime
      testamentary trusts,
      88–90, 94–96
    inheritances and, 7, 88–90,
      99–102
    investment portfolio
      management and, 82
    sale transaction structures
      and, 36–37, 41–42
teaser documents, 33, 34
timing of processes

estate freezes and, 48
overall process of business
    sale, 28–29, 105
presentations to interested
    buyers, 36
release of marketing
    materials, 34
trust between client and
    consultants, 15, 16, 69
trustees
    independent directors for
      advisory boards, 24–26,
      72–73, 75–76
    selection of, 95, 96
    trust structures and,
      20–21
trusts
    business financial planning
      and, 7
    discretionary trusts, 88–90,
      94–96
    need for periodic review of,
      51–52
    required disposition of
      assets, 42–43
    restructuring options for
      sale of company and,
      44–47
    retirement planning and,
      20–21
    shareholders' agreement
      structures and, 73–76
    spousal and family, 94–95
    strategic family wealth
      planning and, 72–73

understanding structure of,
47–50
see also estate freeze

V

value of shares and estate
freezes, 45–46, 48–49
values, 97–98
vision, family businesses and,
4–5, 67
volatility, 31–33

W

wealth
preservation of, 79–80,
84–85, 90

private equity investors
and, 56
tax planning for, 42–43
see also insurance;
investment; strategic
planning
wills
discussing intentions with
beneficiaries of, 88
fairness and equality
concerns, 91–92, 94, 99
strategic family wealth
planning and, 72–73
tax planning and, 42–43
see also estate planning